GW00854155

FIRST ELEMENTS OF GEOGRAPHY

THE BRITISH ISLES

Philip A. Sauvain

HULTON EDUCATIONAL PUBLICATIONS

SOME OTHER BOOKS BY PHILIP SAUVAIN PUBLISHED BY HULTON

Hulton New Geographies
The British Isles
Europe
North America and the USSR
The Developing World
Teachers' Book

Hulton's Practical Geography Series
1. Pictures and Plans
2. Facts, Maps and Places
3. Man and Environment
4. Advanced Techniques and Statistics

Certificate Mapwork

Exploring the World of Man Series (a humanities course)
Man the Farmer
Man the Warrior
Man the Pleasure Lover
Man the Discoverer

Man the Citizen
Man the Thinker
Man the Artist

Breakaway (a social studies course)
People with Problems
Finding a Job and Settling Down
World of Adventure

Vanishing World
Enjoying Ourselves
Where the Money Goes

ACKNOWLEDGEMENTS
The author and publishers are grateful to the following for permission to reproduce photographs:
Aerofilms pp. 30, 31, 39 top, 112, 116, 124; Allan Cash pp. 4, 22, 118; British Broadcasting
Corporation p. 47; Central Electricity Generating Board p. 127; National Coal Board p. 83; Port
of London Authority p. 127; United Kingdom Atomic Energy Authority p. 84.

© 1980 P. A. Sauvain

Cartography: Kirkham Studios
Design and illustration: Pica Design

ISBN 0 7175 0858 7

All rights reserved. No part of this publication
may be reproduced, stored in a retrieval system,
or transmitted in any form or by any means,
electronic, mechanical, photocopying, recording
or otherwise, without the prior written consent of
the copyright holder.

First published 1980 by Hulton Educational Publications Ltd.,
Raans Road, Amersham, Bucks.

Revised and reprinted 1981
Reprinted 1982, 1985

Printed in Great Britain by Martin's of Berwick

CONTENTS

ABOUT MAPS

Directions

One way of describing how to get to a place is to use the directions north, south, east and west. These are called compass directions. Once you know where north is it is easy to find south since this is the opposite direction to north. If you look at the diagram you will see how easy it is to find east and west as well.

On most maps north is usually at the top, south is at the bottom, east is to the right and west is to the left. To make sure it is usual to put a little arrow on the map pointing to north.

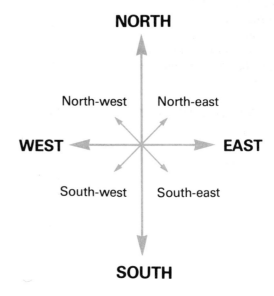

NORTH

North-west   North-east

WEST   EAST

South-west   South-east

SOUTH

N

The directions in between these four main compass points are also shown in the diagram. They are north-east, south-east, south-west and north-west.

Compass directions are very useful to know. You will often come across them in a town. There are streets like South Street and Eastgate and parts of a town like North Lynn and Westminster.

You will often see compass directions in the names of places in Britain. There are towns (Northampton and Southend), rivers (the North Tyne), hills (the Southern Uplands) and counties (West Sussex and East Sussex). There are roads such as the Great North Road and Western Avenue and regions (large areas) of Britain such as East Anglia, the West Country and the South-east.

In fact on a map of a large area like the British Isles compass directions have to be given. It would sound silly if a journey from London to Cardiff was described using words such as; 'turn left when you get into Wales'.

Look at this map of the British Isles. It shows the capital cities of England, Wales, Scotland, Northern Ireland and the Republic of Ireland (Eire).

What is the capital of Wales?
What is the capital of Northern Ireland?
Which capital lies north from Cardiff?
Which capital lies south from Belfast?
Which capital is due west from London?
Which capital city is north-west of London?
Which capital city is in the south-east?
Which is the most northerly capital city?
Which is the most easterly capital city?

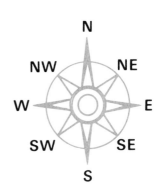

Distances

Another way of saying how to get to a place is to say what the distance is. It is also much easier to follow directions if distances are given as well. 'Turn left and it is about a hundred metres on the right hand side' is much more helpful than 'turn left and it is on the right'.

These distances can be measured on a map if it has been drawn to scale. Drawing a map to scale means that every distance on the map is shown as the same proportion of the real distance on the ground.

In the diagram below you can see that the small line is 1/10th of the size of the longer line. This small line is drawn to a scale showing 1/10th of the real distance. Some maps may be drawn to scales of 1/50 000th of the real distance or even 1/1 000 000th (one millionth) of the real distance on the ground.

The easy way to show a scale on a map is to draw a line scale (called a linear scale). This is a line marked out with a number of equally-spaced shorter distances. Each of these shorter distances is numbered with the length it really represents on the ground.

On a map where the scale is 1/1 000 000th of the real distance a line 100mm long represents 100km on the ground (since one kilometre = one million millimetres). If it is divided into ten equal distances of 10mm, each division then represents 10km on the ground.

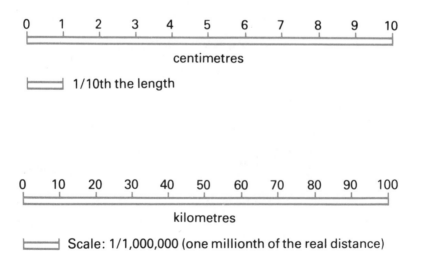

Whenever you have to measure distances on a map look for the line scale. On the next page you can see a map of the British Isles showing some well-known towns and places. The questions ask you to measure the distances between some of these towns.

1. To find the distance between two places on a map put a length of paper with a straight edge on the map so that it joins the two places in a straight line.

2. Mark two dots on this paper opposite the two places on the map.

3. Put the paper against the line scale on the map and find the distance between the two dots you have marked. For instance in the map below the distance between Dublin and Norwich is shown to be 500km.

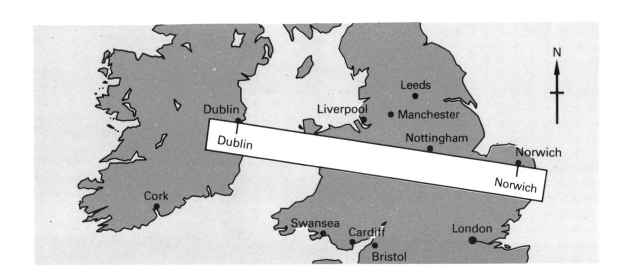

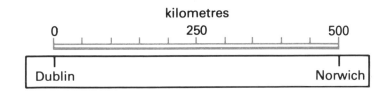

Measure the distances on this map between:

Lerwick and Belfast
London and Edinburgh
Ipswich and Aberdeen
Birmingham and Cardiff
John o'Groats and Lands End
Carlisle and Nottingham
Plymouth and Leeds
Glasgow and Leicester
Newcastle and Liverpool
Swansea and Cambridge
Cork and Inverness
Bristol and Manchester

Lerwick

N

John o'Groats

Inverness

Aberdeen

Edinburgh

Glasgow

Newcastle-upon-Tyne

Belfast

Carlisle

Leeds

Liverpool

Manchester

Dublin

Nottingham

Norwich

Leicester

Birmingham

Cambridge

Ipswich

Cork

Cardiff

London

Swansea

Bristol

Plymouth

Lands End

0   100   200

Km

Showing information on a map

Information can be shown on a map in three main ways.

Some information can be shown as points or dots. On a large scale map the points might represent buildings such as a telephone box or a church. On a small scale map showing a large area the dots might represent villages, railway stations, airports and other important places. The points and dots can be represented by other symbols where a lot of places are to be shown. Squares, circles, small pictures, letters and crosses are often used.

Some information has to be shown as lines. Different types of lines can be shown by using colours, different thicknesses, double lines and broken lines. Lines are used to show roads, railways, canals, rivers and boundaries between countries and counties.

Some information can best be shown as areas or patches of different colours or different types of shading. They are used to show woodland, lakes, the sea, a large town, a park, orchards and other areas.

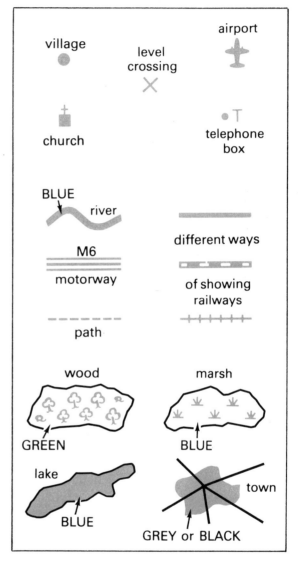

Look at the map below. It shows a railway line, a station and a wood.

How are these three bits of information shown on this map?

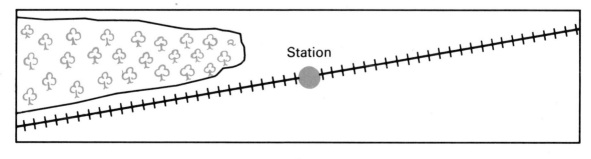

9

How height is shown on a map

Surveyors find the height of a hill by measuring the difference between the highest point (the summit) and sea level. The highest point in Britain is the summit of Ben Nevis in Scotland. It is 1392 metres above sea level.

Heights like this can be shown written out in full on a map. The trouble is that if a large number of heights are shown the map is very confusing. It does not give any idea of how the land slopes up and down.

A better way is to use lines called contours. Contour lines join places which are the same height above sea level. The 100 metre contour line on the map opposite joins all the places which are 100 metres above sea level. The 200 metre contour line joins all the places which are 200 metres above sea level and the 300 metre contour line joins all those places which are 300 metres above sea level. From this map we know that all the land within the 300 metres

contour line is over 300 metres in height. If it was lower than this it would be between the other contour lines on the map.

Contour maps often seem complicated. In hilly areas there are lots of contour lines. To make the maps simpler to look at it is sometimes easier just to take two or three contours and colour or shade the different heights between them. When you look at a map like this the shaded or coloured areas quickly tell you where the higher land is.

As you can see in the map opposite the three main methods of showing information on a map can all be used to show the height of the land. *Dots* give the height of certain points (these are called spot heights). *Lines* joining places which are the same height above sea level are called contours. Coloured or shaded *areas* show land above or below a certain height.

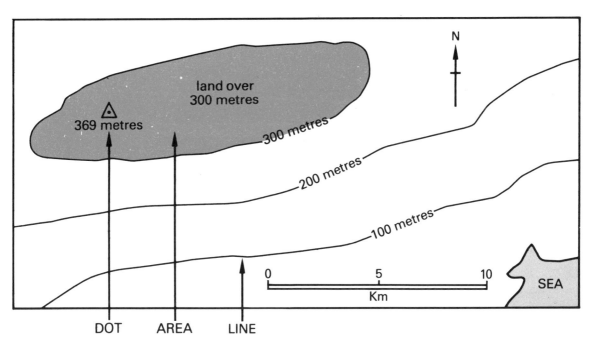

land over
300 metres

369 metres

N

300 metres

200 metres

100 metres

SEA

0   5   10
Km

DOT   AREA   LINE

▲
Which is the highest part of the area shown in this map? Is it in the north-east, north-west, south-west or south-east? What height is it? Copy the map and colour in all the land which is lower than 100 metres in height.

Copy the map below. Choose three colours and use the darkest colour to show the land over 400 metres. Use the next colour to show land between 200 and 400 metres in height. Use the lightest colour to show land below 200 metres.
▼

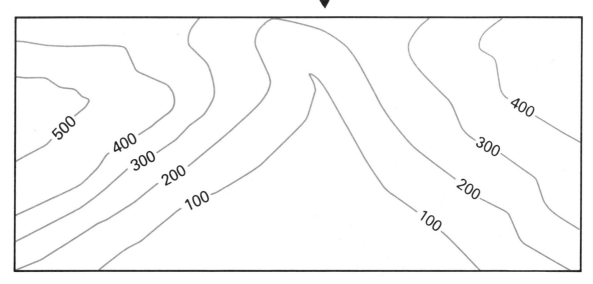

500

400

300

200

100

400

300

200

100

In the map below you can see a map of northern Scotland. The map shows contour lines at 200 metres and at 500 metres above sea level. Different shades of colours have been used to show the areas between these lines. The darker shading has been used for the higher land. The letters A, B, C, D, E and F mark three different types of land.

1. Which letters mark the highest land of all?

2. Which letters mark lowland areas under **200 metres** in height?

3. Which letters mark land between 200 and 500 metres in height?

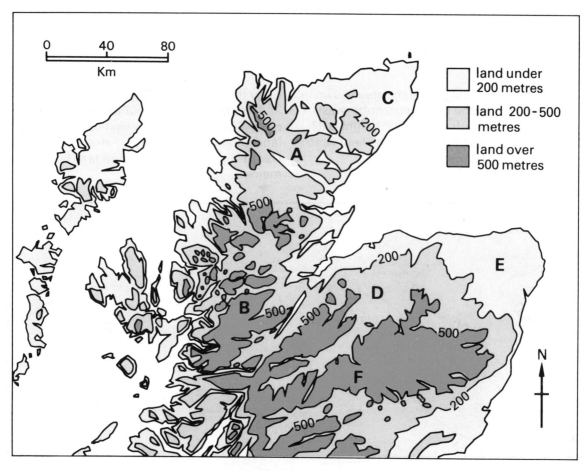

Exercises

1. What are the eight main compass points?

2. What is the opposite of (a) south (b) north-west (c) east?

3. Which side of a map usually faces north?

4. How is north usually shown on a map?

5. Complete this sentence:
   On a map drawn to scale every distance shown on the map ....

6. What is a linear scale?

7. Give one example of the type of information which can be shown on a map by each of the following (a) dots (b) areas (c) lines.

8. Complete this sentence:
   Contour lines join places which are ....

9. Look at the map below showing part of Europe. Use compass directions to fill in the blanks.
   Cork is in.........ern Eire. Antwerp in Belgium is.........of London and.........of Amsterdam in Holland. Aberdeen is on the.........ern coast of Scotland. London is.........from Paris and.........from Oslo.

10. How far is it from London to (a) Paris (b) Oslo (c) Amsterdam (d) Aberdeen?

11. How are the towns shown on this map? How are the countries shown?

12. In which part of Europe are the British Isles situated?

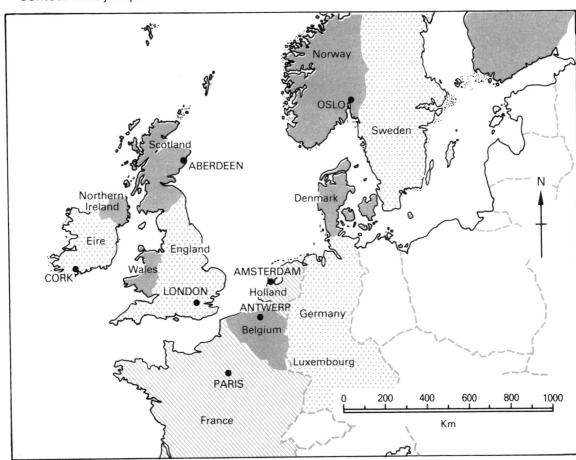

THE POSITION OF BRITAIN

England is in the United Kingdom, in Great Britain and in the British Isles. These are the names for different groups of countries. Great Britain is the chief island (or mainland) of the British Isles and is divided into three countries – England, Wales and Scotland. The United Kingdom includes all the four countries governed from Westminster. These are England, Wales, Scotland and Northern Ireland. In addition the Channel Islands and the Isle of Man are linked to the United Kingdom although having their own governments. The British Isles is the name given to all of these islands and countries – England, Wales, Scotland, Northern Ireland, Eire (the Republic of Ireland).

People living in the British Isles have many advantages.

1. They live in an area affected by the warm North Atlantic Drift or Gulf Stream. This is a warm ocean current in the Atlantic Ocean. It brings warm waters from the Gulf of Mexico into the cold seas of the North Atlantic. Because it is warm it keeps the ports of Britain free from ice in the winter It also helps to make the weather milder than would otherwise be expected in a group of islands so far north (50°N to 60°N). In Canada the St. Lawrence River is frozen over in winter although it is further south (and nearer the Equator) than any part of Britain.

2. The islands of the British Isles have a very long coastline. There are many ports. Some face Europe and some face North America. No other countries in Europe are quite so well placed to trade with the countries of the world.

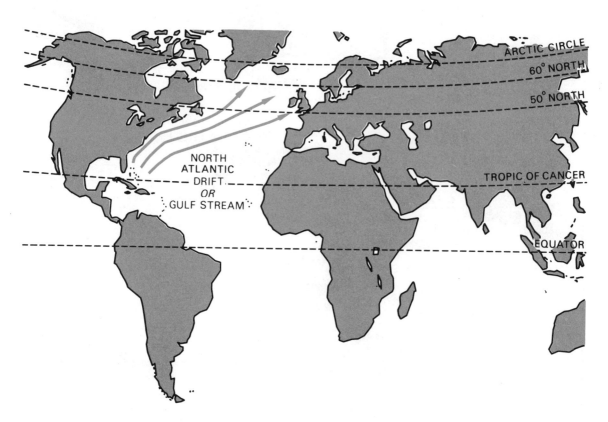

3. There were rich minerals in Britain in the past which helped to make Britain the world's first industrial nation. Today there are still rich deposits of coal whilst oil and gas are important new sources of energy found under the British part of the North Sea.

4. Much of southern and eastern Britain is good farmland.

5. As an island it has not been invaded by an enemy from Europe since 1066. Almost all of the other countries of Europe have been invaded at some time in the last 250 years. Britain was able to defy Napoleon nearly two hundred years ago and Hitler between 1939 and 1945.

This map will help you to understand the position of the British Isles in relation to the other countries of Europe.

Compared to the other 14 countries of Western Europe, shown on the map on page 15, the United Kingdom

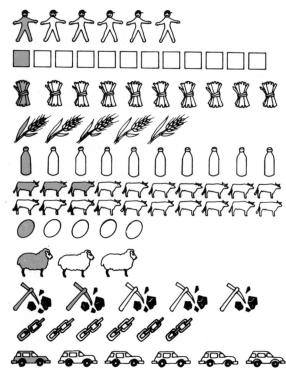

has 17% of the population (17 people in 100 or roughly 1 in every 6)

has 8% of the area (8 hectares in every 100 hectares or roughly 1 in every 12)

grows 10% of the wheat (1 tonne in every 10 tonnes)

grows 20% of the barley (1 tonne in every 5 tonnes)

produces 10% of the milk (1 litre in every 10 litres)

produces 15% of the beef (3kg in every 20kg)

produces 20% of the eggs (1 egg in every 5 eggs)

produces 33% of the lamb and mutton (1/3rd of Europe's mutton and lamb)

mines 40% of the coal (2 tonnes in every 5 tonnes)

makes 16% of the steel (1 tonne in every 6 tonnes)

makes 16% of the cars (1 car in every 6 cars)

The United Kingdom has the second highest percentage of people living in towns and has the largest city (London) in Europe.

It has the lowest percentage of people employed in agriculture, the busiest international airport (Heathrow, London) and the most crowded roads after the Netherlands.

Look at the statements below. Which statements are TRUE and which are FALSE? Write the statements out so that they all read correctly.

1. For its size the United Kingdom has over twice as many people living there than do the countries which together make up the rest of Western Europe.

2. 1/5th of the eggs and 1/3rd of the lamb and mutton of Western Europe are produced in the United Kingdom.

3. The United Kingdom has the largest percentage of people working in agriculture in Europe.

4. Britain is one of the two largest producers of coal in Western Europe.

Exercises

1. Which countries form the United Kingdom?

2. What name can be given to England, Wales and Scotland?

3. What two countries make up Ireland?

4. Why are the ports of Britain free from ice in winter?

5. Where is the best farmland in Britain?

6. When was the last major invasion of Britain?

7. What advantages are there in living in a large group of islands like the British Isles? What are the disadvantages?

8. Look at the map below. Find out the names of the
    (a) islands numbered 1, 2, 3
    (b) seas numbered 4, 5
    (c) stretch of water numbered 6
    (d) countries numbered 7, 8, 9, 10, 11, 12

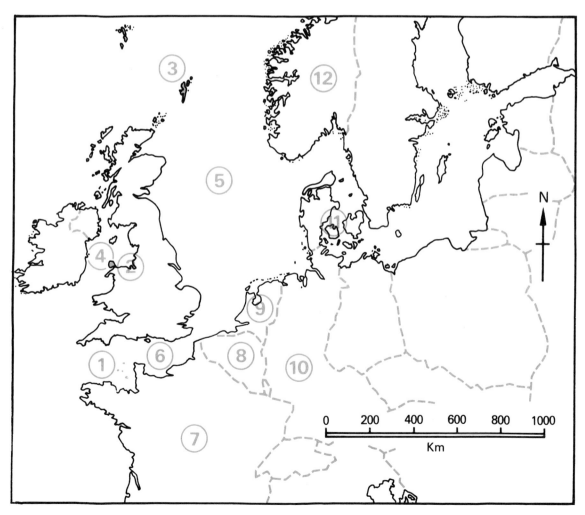

THE LAND
Rocks

Volcanoes could have been seen in Britain many millions of years ago.

Deep beneath the surface of the earth the rocks are very hot indeed and as a result are in a liquid (molten) form. Where there is a crack or weakness in the earth's surface this molten rock, called lava, flows out over the surrounding land forming a volcano. Sometimes the lava comes up with great force and it is accompanied by explosions. Rocks and ashes shoot out from the centre of the volcano (called its crater). The lava then spills out over the rocks and ashes. After a time the volcano goes quiet. The lava cools and becomes solid. Rocks formed in these ways are known as volcanic rocks.

In Scotland, Ireland, Wales, the Lake District, Cornwall, Devon and other areas volcanic rock can be seen today. Many hills and mountains are made up largely of volcanic rocks.

Some hills are made up of sedimentary rocks. Sedimentary rocks are formed from other rocks or from the remains of plants and creatures. When rain fell on the land it washed channels in the hillsides. Some channels widened and got deeper and became river valleys. The rock which was washed and cut away was taken by the river to the sea. Gradually the bits of rock got worn down to grains of sand and mud. At the end of the river (its mouth) the sand and mud floated down to the bottom of the sea floor.

After millions of years these sands and muds were piled high in layers. Each layer weighed down and pressed the layers below turning them after a long time into hard rocks. The layers of sand became sandstone, layers of mud became clay. The sediments of sand and clay are like the sediments (dregs) of coffee which settle at the bottom of a mug if it is not stirred. Eventually when the sea level went down or the land was lifted by movement of the earth, these rocks formed part of the land.

Some sedimentary rocks were formed from the shells and skeletons of sea creatures who lived in warm seas millions of years ago. These shells and skeletons helped to form the limestones of northern England and the chalk of southern England.

Other sedimentary rocks were formed from trees and plants which rotted away in swamps millions of years ago when Britain's climate was much hotter than it is now. Later the rotting trees and plants were pressed down to form layers of coal. These layers are called seams.

Sometimes the rocks were pushed up into mountains by movements of the earth. This is called folding. Sometimes there were earthquakes and the surface of the earth was cracked (faulted) and lifted up. Many of the hills we see today were first formed in these ways.

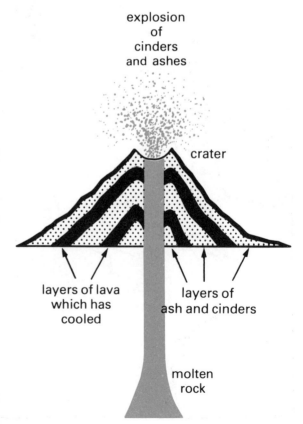

explosion of cinders and ashes

crater

layers of lava which has cooled

layers of ash and cinders

molten rock

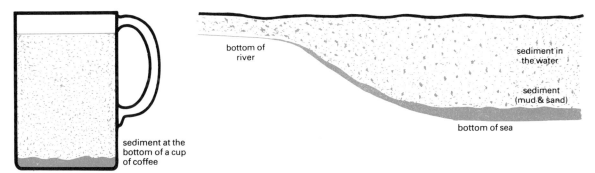

sediment at the bottom of a cup of coffee

bottom of river

sediment in the water

sediment (mud & sand)

bottom of sea

Folded rocks

Look at the statements below. Which statements are TRUE and which are FALSE? Write the statements out so that they all read correctly.

1. Coal is a volcanic rock.

2. Sedimentary rocks are formed when lava cools.

3. Limestone is formed from rotting plants and trees.

4. The centre of a volcano is called a crater.

Where can you see volcanic rocks in Britain today?

19

Soils

Soil was formed out of the rocks. If you dig really deep down in some areas you come across rocks which are broken. Deeper down you reach the solid rock (called bedrock). You can sometimes see these layers of rock in a cliff side at the coast or in a quarry.

It took thousands of years to form soil. Rain, frost, heat and sun made the rock's surface crack and break up. Plants grew in the cracks. As the rock broke up further leaves, stalks and roots mixed with the broken rock. Worms and creatures mixed it up even more as they moved through it. It was a very very slow process. It might have taken a thousand years to make a layer of soil about the depth of the length of your thumb.

The layer of soil on the top is called top soil. Soils affect the way in which the land can be farmed and the types of plants which can be grown there.

Since the soils come from the rocks you can see that the type of rock in an area plays a big part in the formation of soil. The weather also affects the way in which soil is formed. Soils in the highlands often come from hard volcanic rocks which take a long time to break up. There is heavy rainfall in these hills and this tends to make the mountain soils thin and very poor. Few plants grow well in them. There is much moorland and peat bog. Lowland soils are usually deeper and better for growing crops.

Some soils are very sticky in wet weather. These are clay soils. They are rich enough to grow plants in but because they get muddy and hold a lot of water they are often left as fields of grassland.

Very sandy soils are full of little stones and pieces of grit. Rain water goes right through them. They are usually poor soils for plants and are often left as areas of heathland and woodland. Other soils on harder sandstones are richer and much more suitable for growing crops.

Good soils are somewhere in between the sticky clay soils and the very sandy soils. They do not get muddy in wet weather but do hold enough water for the plants. They have a crumbly feel to them and if you picked up a handful you would see bits of plants in it. This is humus. It is leaves and stalks which have rotted. The goodness in the old leaves can now be used again by new plants. It is the ideal thing to find in the soil if you are a gardener or farmer. This is why gardeners often make a compost heap out of lawn cuttings, leaves and kitchen waste. They let it rot and then add it to the soil to help the plants grow. Farmers use manure from the cowsheds, henhouses and piggeries.

1. Copy the picture below.
2. What is sub-soil?
3. What name is given to the soil which lies on top of the sub-soil?
4. What is humus?
5. Name four things you would expect to find in a spadeful of soil.
6. Which soils are sticky when wet?

What is in the soil?

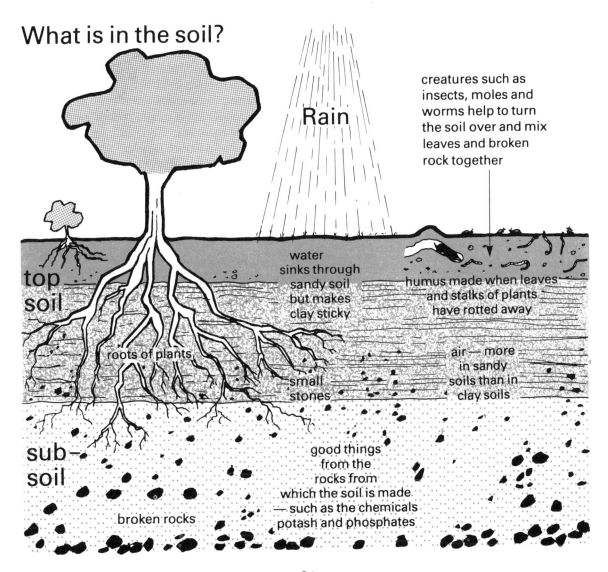

Rain

creatures such as insects, moles and worms help to turn the soil over and mix leaves and broken rock together

top soil

water sinks through sandy soil but makes clay sticky

humus made when leaves and stalks of plants have rotted away

roots of plants

small stones

air — more in sandy soils than in clay soils

sub-soil

good things from the rocks from which the soil is made — such as the chemicals potash and phosphates

broken rocks

Hills of Britain

The map on the opposite page shows the main hills and mountains of the British Isles. As you can see the mountains over 500 metres high are in Scotland, Ireland, Wales, the Pennines, West Country and the English Lake District. They are all in the north or west. This area of high land is often called Highland Britain.

Most of the really high mountains are in Scotland where the highest mountains are in the Grampians. A group of mountains covering an area is usually called a range. The Grampian range of mountains is well over 1000 metres in height in places. To the north-west of the Grampians lie the North West Highlands and much further to the south there are the Southern Uplands. However between the Grampians and the Southern Uplands, you can see a wide lowland area. This is where, Glasgow, Aberdeen, Edinburgh and Dundee and most of the other large towns of Scotland are situated.

A very large part of Wales is hill or mountain country. The highest mountains are in the north-west. The highest mountain here is Snowdon and the area round about is usually called Snowdonia.

Ireland is often said to be like a saucer! Almost all of its hills and mountains are round the edge. There are the mountains of Donegal, Antrim and Mourne in the north and those of Kerry and Wicklow in the south.

In England the main highland areas are the Cumbrian Mountains in the Lake District and the Pennines in the north and Dartmoor, Bodmin Moor and Exmoor in Devon and Cornwall.

In Lowland Britain there are still many hills but they are lower than those mentioned being under 300 metres or so in height. Many of them are formed from chalk or limestone. Chalk is a white rock which is easily recognised. The chalk hills have rounded outlines and make up the North and South Downs, the Chilterns, the downland of Dorset, Wiltshire and Hampshire, and the wolds of Yorkshire and Lincolnshire. The chief limestone hills are those of the Cotswolds and the North York Moors.

Hay Tor Dartmoor

Copy the map on this page.

Mark with a dot the position of your town or village (or that of a town or village where a relative lives).

Which is the nearest range of hills to the town or village you have marked on the map? Is it in highland or lowland Britain?

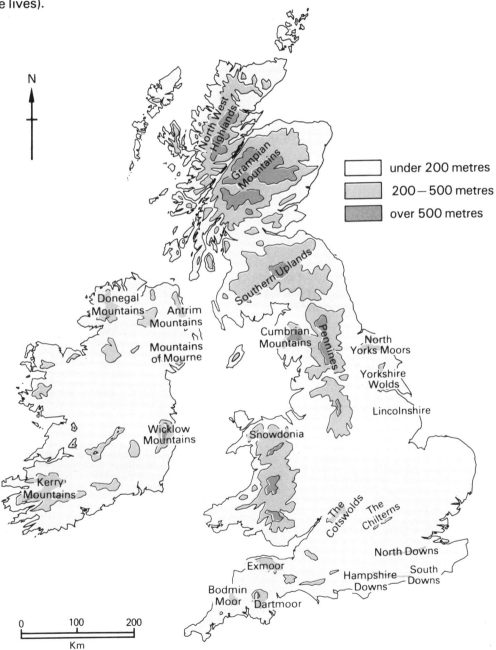

N

North West Highlands

Grampian Mountains

under 200 metres

200 – 500 metres

over 500 metres

Southern Uplands

Donegal Mountains

Antrim Mountains

Mountains of Mourne

Cumbrian Mountains

Pennines

North Yorks Moors

Yorkshire Wolds

Lincolnshire

Wicklow Mountains

Snowdonia

Kerry Mountains

The Cotswolds

The Chilterns

North Downs

Exmoor

Hampshire Downs

South Downs

Bodmin Moor

Dartmoor

0   100   200

Km

If you walked across England from White-haven to Scarborough you would have to climb the mountains of the Lake District first of all, then the Pennine Hills and finally the hills of the North York Moors. Your journey might look like this.

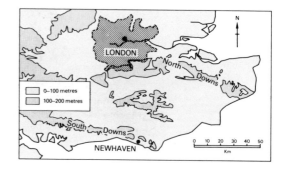

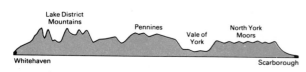

A picture diagram like this is called a section. The height of the land is exaggerated in this type of diagram.

Look at the two maps on the right.

1. What hills would you have to climb if you walked (a) from Padstow to Torquay (b) from London to Newhaven?

2. Draw pictures (sections) like the one above to show roughly what the hills look like (a) between Padstow and Torquay, and (b) between London and Newhaven.

3. Write a few words to describe these journeys. Is the land hilly or lowland?

4. Which would be the easier journey to do?

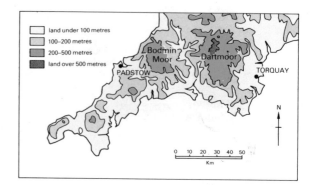

Slopes and features

These pictures help to explain some of the names used to describe different types of hill or valley.

A hill or mountain which is flat or fairly level on top (at the summit) is called a PLATEAU.

A flat or fairly level area of low land is called a PLAIN. The flat floor of a river valley which floods after heavy rain is called its FLOOD PLAIN (see also page 35).

A valley with very steep sides is called a GORGE.

A valley without a river is called a DRY VALLEY.

A hill top with steep slopes on either side is called a RIDGE.

A small hill standing by itself is called a KNOLL.

A gap between two hills is called a COL or a SADDLE.

Write a sentence to describe what you can see in each of these photographs.

When people say what hills and valleys look like they often use special words to describe the things they see. Words like rugged, craggy, stony, rocky and uneven help to describe the rocks on the slopes of a mountain. Other words say how steep a slope is, such as overhanging, precipitous, sheer, sloping and gently sloping. Some places can be said to be flat or level. Some land has slopes with gentle, smooth and rounded outlines. It goes up and down and is called rolling or undulating land.

The word landscape is often used to describe a type of country or a view. This usually means hills, valleys, woods and fields but it can also mean towns, factories and roads.

There are several different types of landscape in Britain. Often the differences are because of the rocks below, as you have already seen. The biggest differences are in the way the land is used and the way it slopes.

The height and steepness of the slopes have had an effect on the way in which people live. They have affected the way in which villages and towns have grown, how many farmers have farmed the land, the direction taken by roads, railways and canals or where houses have been built in a town. They also have an effect on the weather and on the plants and animals that can be found on the slopes.

Write two sentences to describe the landscape you can see in this photograph. Where are the houses situated?

Look at the picture below.

1. How have the slopes shown affected the way in which people live? Make a list of all the different things you can see in this picture which tell you about the effect of hills and slopes on the way in which people live.

2. Write down the words you would use to describe the slopes shown in the picture.

3. What names can be given to the features shown by the letters A, B, C, D, E?

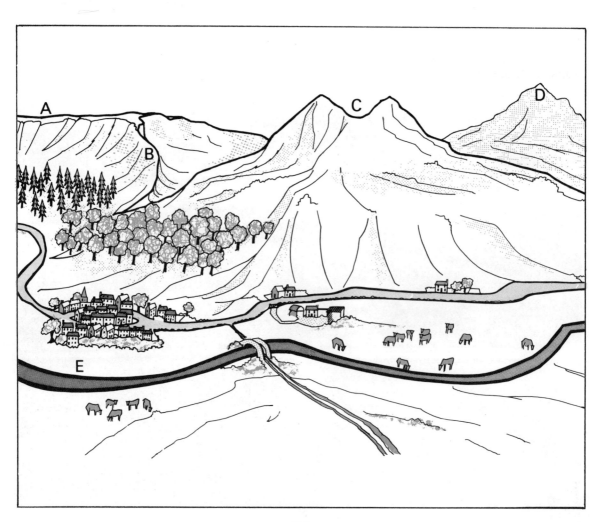

Chalk and Limestone

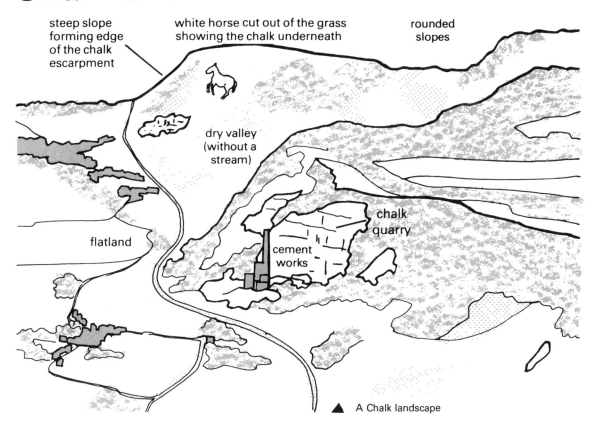

steep slope forming edge of the chalk escarpment

white horse cut out of the grass showing the chalk underneath

rounded slopes

dry valley (without a stream)

chalk quarry

flatland

cement works

▲ A Chalk landscape

▼ A limestone pothole

If you walked on the South Downs, the Chilterns, the Mendips near Bristol or the Pennine Hills near Sheffield you might be surprised to notice that there are hardly any streams or rivers to be seen on the hills. This is because the rocks which form these hills allow water to sink right through them. The rocks are said to be permeable.

Chalk (rather like blackboard chalk) soaks water up whilst Carboniferous Limestone lets the water seep or drip through cracks and joints in the rock. The water eats away at the limestone and dissolves it (this is why water taken from limestone areas is always hard). The cracks and joints get bigger and form potholes and caves. Many potholes can be seen in the Carboniferous Limestone hills of Britain such as those near Settle in Yorkshire or Castleton in Derbyshire.

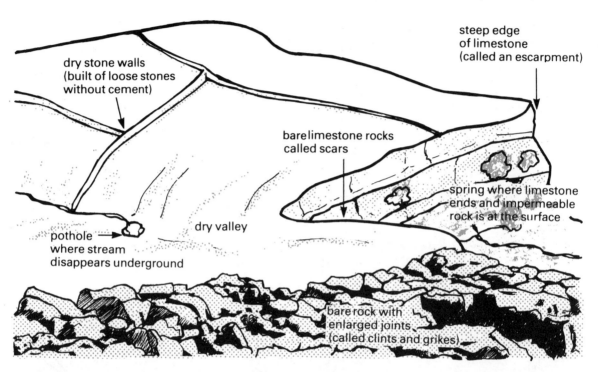

dry stone walls (built of loose stones without cement)

steep edge of limestone (called an escarpment)

bare limestone rocks called scars

spring where limestone ends and impermeable rock is at the surface

pothole where stream disappears underground

dry valley

bare rock with enlarged joints (called clints and grikes)

The pictures on this page and the previous page show some of the things to be seen in Chalk and Carboniferous Limestone country.

What features are shown in the photograph below? Was it taken in Chalk or Carboniferous Limestone country? Give your reasons.

Water supplies

We cannot live long without water. As you have seen rain falling on chalk and limestone areas usually sinks or seeps through the surface of the ground and into the rocks. This is the water which is found when a well is dug. Pumps bring this underground water to the surface. Some underground water comes naturally to the surface as springs.

Many towns take their water from reservoirs. Where possible these reservoirs are built across deep valleys in the hills. This is because a deep valley when dammed can hold back a lot of water. A wide shallow valley has to be flooded over a much bigger area to hold the same amount of water. Moreover the hills of Britain get more rain than the lowlands. There is less chance of the reservoirs in the hills drying up completely in a summer of hot dry weather.

Water from huge reservoirs in the hills is taken by pipeline to the cities of England. Birmingham gets water from Wales and Manchester gets water from the Lake District.

The Derwent Reservoir in the Peak District.

Exercises

1. What are rocks formed from molten lava called?

2. How are sedimentary rocks formed?

3. Name these sedimentary rocks:
   (a) it gets sticky when wet
   (b) it was formed from sands
   (c) it is white and soaks up water like a sponge
   (d) it can be dissolved by rainwater

4. Complete this sentence:
   Highland Britain is in the .... and ....
   Lowland Britain is in the .... and the ....

5. Where does soil come from?

6. Name three things which help soil to form.

7. How have the height and steepness of slopes had an effect on the way in which people live?

8. Write these sentences out in full and fill in the blanks:
   A ridge is a hill with .... A .... is a steepsided valley. An upland area with a flat or nearly level summit is called a .... A col or .... is a .... between two hills. A plain is a ....

9. Look at this map.
   Find out the names of the hills and mountains which have been marked and labelled with their first letters. Write these names out in full.

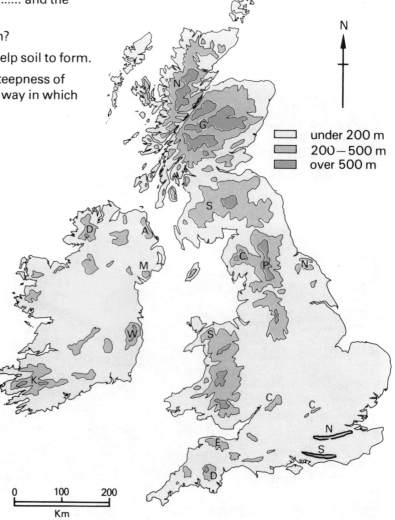

under 200 m
200 – 500 m
over 500 m

VALLEYS
River Valleys

When rain falls it collects in pools, puddles and small streams. Most of it finds its way into a river and then flows back into the sea. In a storm the heavy rain washes soil into the streams. When the rivers are nearly bursting their banks they flow so strongly that rocks and pebbles are whirled along and bang against the sides (banks) and against the bottom (the bed) of the river. This loosens stones and even helps to wear down rocks. This wearing away of the river is called erosion.

Over thousands of years the valleys get deeper and wider. The soil and rocks eroded from the land are washed downstream (towards the sea) and deposited as sediments. In this way rivers help to shape the valleys in which they flow.

Rivers always flow downhill even though the slope of the river may be very gentle indeed. In a river in lowland Britain you would not be able to see the slope although you would be able to see in which direction the river was flowing. On a highland river the slope is often easy to see — especially when it is marked by waterfalls and small rapids as you can see on page 35.

In the map you can see some of the names which are given to the different parts of a river.

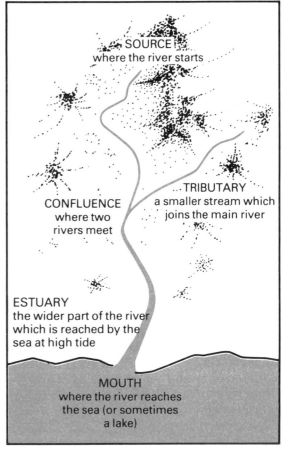

SOURCE
where the river starts

CONFLUENCE
where two
rivers meet

TRIBUTARY
a smaller stream which
joins the main river

ESTUARY
the wider part of the river
which is reached by the
sea at high tide

MOUTH
where the river reaches
the sea (or sometimes
a lake)

These pictures show some of the things which can sometimes be seen in the valley of a river or stream.

In the hills the rivers flow quickly and there are waterfalls and lots of stones and boulders (large rocks) in the river. They stand on the bed of the river.

There are usually lots of deep pools in these highland rivers and many small waterfalls called rapids. Sometimes there are holes in the rocks on the bed of the river. These potholes, as they are called, have been formed by the river swirling round pebbles in holes in the rock and making them bigger.

In many valleys the river often winds and bends. This is called meandering. Rivers often meander and flow slowly in a wide valley. The valley floor on either side of the river may be flat. This is because the river occasionally floods. After days of rain the river bursts its banks and the floodwater covers the bottom of the valley leaving mud everywhere. The mud is called alluvium. In the past it might have flooded often and over thousands of years a thick layer of this alluvium was formed covering the valley floor and making it flat. This flat area is called the flood plain.

Near the mouth of the river the sea comes in at high tide. This part of the river is called the estuary. At low tide you can often see thick mud banks here and on the bed of the river.

1. What features are shown in the photographs on the opposite page?
2. What name is given to the bottom of a river? What is the name given to the sides of the river?
3. Is the source of a river downsteam or up-stream?
4. Do rivers flow uphill or downhill?
5. If you were in a canoe on a river which flowed into the sea how would you know which direction to paddle in to reach the mouth of the river?

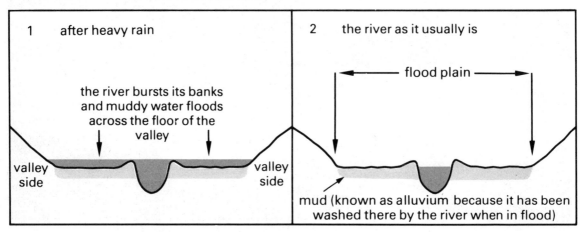

1   after heavy rain

the river bursts its banks and muddy water floods across the floor of the valley

valley side

valley side

2   the river as it usually is

← flood plain →

mud (known as alluvium because it has been washed there by the river when in flood)

Rivers of Britain

Valleys are very important as places in which to live. The people who live there usually build their homes away from the flat valley floor where it is likely to flood. Nowadays many flood plains have been drained to try to make the land dry. In the past it was marshland and frequently under water.

Draining a low-lying area usually means digging long ditches and putting pipes under the fields. Water sinks through the soil and into these pipes and flows into the ditches. In this way the land is drained of water.

Towns, villages and farms usually avoid steep slopes on the sides of the valley. Somewhere just above the flood plain is the usual place for a village. This is also the best place for roads and railway lines.

Rivers have to be crossed. If there is no bridge the people on either side of the river are divided from one another. The crossing points are therefore very important. They often become the places where important towns and villages grow up.

The valley is also a place where factories have been built. In the past water power was often used to turn machines. When steam was used water was taken from the river to make steam. Rivers were also useful places in which to get rid of waste and rubbish.

The map opposite shows the main British rivers. Because Britain is relatively small there are no really long rivers. The longest river is the Shannon in Ireland. In England and Wales the longest river is the Severn. It rises in the hills of Wales and its estuary lies between Wales and England where it empties into the Bristol Channel.

Copy the map. Mark on it with a dot the position of your home town or village (or that of a town or village where a relative lives). Which is the nearest river on the map to the town or village you have marked?

36

N

Spey

Dee

Tay

Forth

NORTH SEA

Clyde

Tweed

Tyne

Wear

Eden

Tees

Swale

Ouse

Aire

Humber

IRISH SEA

Don

Mersey

Dee

Trent

Shannon

Nene

Gt.Ouse

Severn

Wye

Usk

Thames

Exe

Tamar

0	100	200

Km

Valleys cut by ice

About 20 000 years ago a visitor to the Scottish Highlands, Snowdonia or the Lake District would have seen glaciers in the highland valleys. At one time the whole of Britain north of the Thames and the Bristol Channel was covered by ice.

Glaciers are like rivers of ice. They are formed when the climate is cold in summer as well as in winter. When the winter snows do not melt in the summer they collect and form ice. This ice flows slowly down the slopes of the hills. These are the glaciers which once cut deep valleys in the highlands of Britain. Similar glaciers are cutting deep valleys today in the Alps and in the Himalayas.

Glaciers deepen their valleys and also widen and straighten them. They do this when stones and rocks which have fallen on to the glacier or have become attached to the bottom and sides scrape other earth away as the glacier flows slowly down the valley. This earth is carried along together with the huge boulders which are sometimes loosened high in the hills and which fall on to the surface of the glacier. Eventually the glacier reaches a point where the summer weather is warm enough to melt the ice. The earth and stones are dropped at the end of the glacier (its snout) and form a ridge of earth stretching right across the valley like a dam wall.

When the weather generally becomes warmer the glaciers and ice sheets gradually melt and many other stones, boulders and piles of earth are left behind as the ice disappears. Sometimes the streams and rivers which flow into the valley after the melting of the ice cannot escape to the sea and form lakes dammed by the earth. The earth and stones left behind by a glacier is called moraine. The moraine at the end of the glacier is called a terminal (end) moraine. Where piles of earth and stones have been dropped beneath an ice sheet they form rounded hills called drumlins. The stones and boulders moved by the ice over large distances are called erratics.

The diagram below and the photograph show some of the different features formed by glaciers which can be seen in the highlands of Britain today—over 10 000 years since the ice melted away.

deep circular hollows in the hills where ice collected (called corries)

where the glacier scraped it left a smooth sided U shaped valley

hanging valleys where the ice did not erode as rapidly as in the main valley

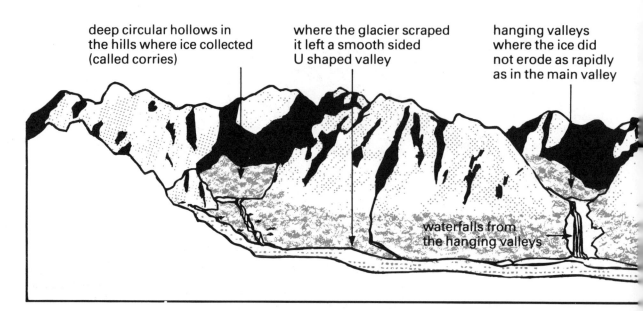

waterfalls from the hanging valleys

What features shown in the diagram are also shown in the photograph above?

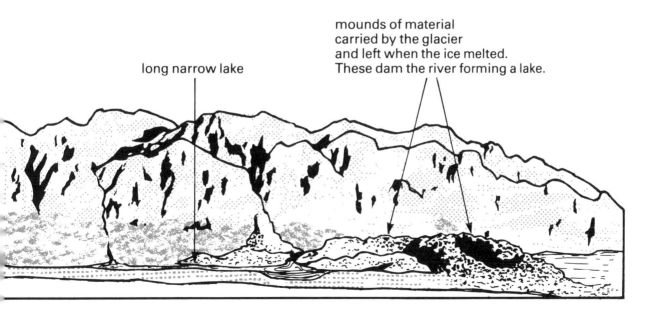

long narrow lake

mounds of material
carried by the glacier
and left when the ice melted.
These dam the river forming a lake.

Exercises

1. What is the name given to streams which join a main river?

2. What is the name for the place where (a) a river starts (b) two rivers meet (c) a river reaches the sea?

3. Complete these sentences:
   Rivers always flow ....hill. Rivers wear away the valleys in which they flow. This is called .... In .... areas the rivers are usually fast-flowing and have many .... in their beds. There are often w..........s and p..........s. In lowland areas rivers often .... from side to side. The flat valley floor is often covered with .... This is called the .... plain.

4. What river features are shown in these pictures?

5. Name three rivers which flow into the North Sea.

6. Name three rivers which flow into the Irish Sea.

7. Name five features to be seen in a mountain area which was once carved out by glaciers.

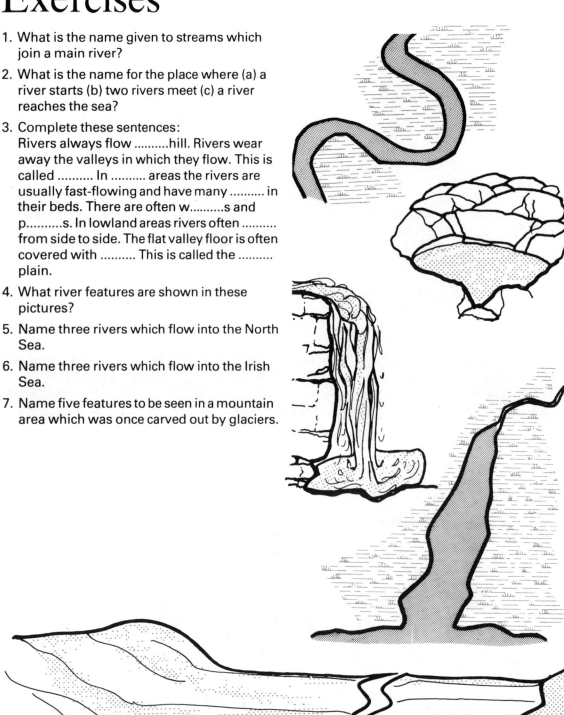

THE COAST

Many stretches of the British coastline are under attack from the sea. When the sea comes in at high tide the waves break on the beaches. Sometimes they cut away rock at the bottom of a cliff. The cliff collapses and the pieces of rock are washed away. These pieces of rock gradually wear down into small pebbles and eventually become grains of sand. This sand is often piled up by the sea at another part of the coast as a sandy beach.

Some cliffs (like those in the photograph below) are of hard rock and not easily washed away. Other cliffs are of soft rock and easily eroded. In parts of East Anglia, villages which were built nine hundred years ago have been washed away and now lie under the waves over a kilometre away from the present day shore.

Pages 42-43 show some of the things you can expect to see at the seaside. The waves do the damage because they wash up pebbles.

When a breaker crashes with stones in it the pebbles help to cut away (erode) the rock.

In hard rock the cliff can be cut away without the rock above collapsing immediately. In this type of rock you can expect to find caves. When a cave is cut right through it makes a natural arch. Sometimes a part of the cliff or headland is separated from the rest of the cliff and stands as a small island in the sea. This is called a stack.

Rocks which have been worn away by the sea become pebbles, grains of sand or mud. These are carried by the waves to become beaches and mud banks at other places along the coastline. Sometimes the sea washes up so much mud, sand and pebbles that it becomes new land. This is often the reason why marshes are found along the coast.

Some towns which were ports five hundred years ago are now some distance away from the sea. Their harbours or estuaries have been filled with sand and mud.

Describe what you can
see in each of the
photographs on these
two pages and also on
page 41.

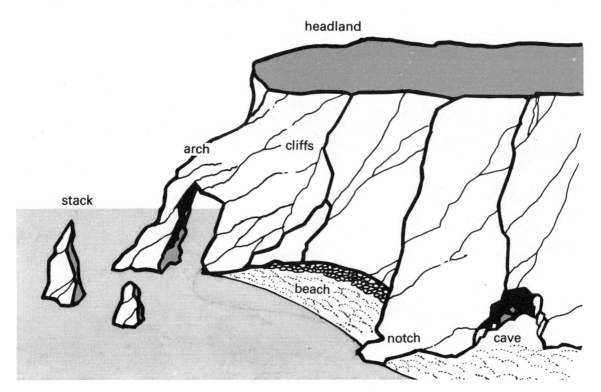

headland

arch

cliffs

stack

beach

notch

cave

43

Coasts of Britain

Britain has a very long coastline. This is because there are over 1000 islands and because
there are many bays and long winding estuaries.

    The map below shows some of the most
interesting features of the coastline of Britain.

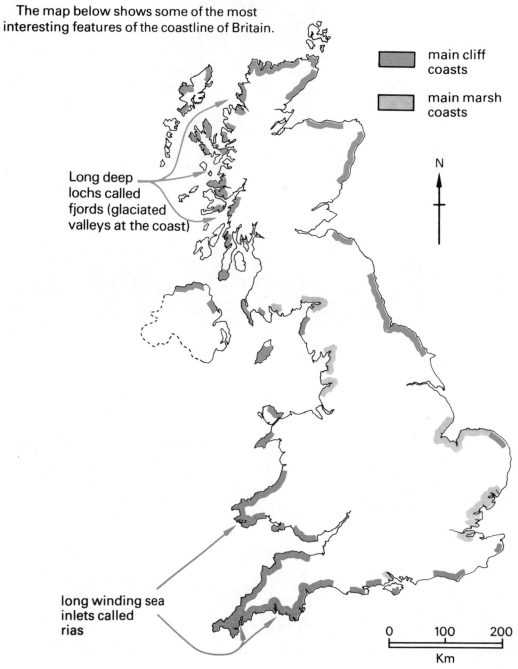

main cliff
coasts

main marsh
coasts

N

Long deep
lochs called
fjords (glaciated
valleys at the coast)

long winding sea
inlets called
rias

0   100   200

Km

Exercises

1. What causes cliffs to be worn away (eroded)?

2. Look at the photograph. Where have the pebbles and the sand come from? What shape are the pebbles? Why are they shaped like this?

3. Why has Britain got a very long coastline?

4. What is the name given to an island of rock cut away from a cliff?

5. Copy the picture on this page and name the features marked, 1, 2, 3, 4, 5, 6.

6. Where in the United Kingdom could you see (a) fjords (b) rias (c) marshes at the coast (d) long cliff coastlines?

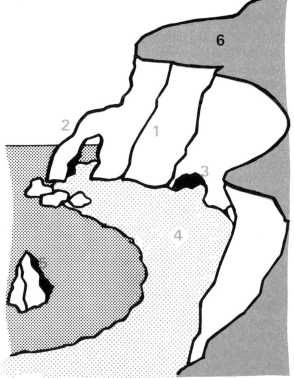

45

THE WEATHER

For most of the time the weather in Britain is mild when compared with the weather in other countries. British summers are hardly ever very hot and the winters are hardly ever very cold. Drought (when there is no rain for a long period) does not occur very often. Only occasionally are there terrible natural disasters such as the flooding of towns or landslides.

The reason for this is because Britain is a group of islands close to the Atlantic Ocean. It is surrounded by water. Few places are far from the sea. The sea always takes a long time to go cold and this affects the temperatures in Britain in winter. However it also takes a long time to get warm and this affects the temperatures in summer.

The North Atlantic Drift (see page 14) brings warmer waters to the shores of Britain than would be normally expected so far north of the Equator. Normally the weather is colder the nearer you are to the North Pole (in the Northern Hemisphere) and warmer the nearer you are to the Equator.

The hills and mountains of Britain also affect the weather. The temperatures are cooler and there is more rain in the hilly districts.

Britain is also affected by the movement of large masses of air. There is cold air to the north (POLAR AIR) and warm air to the south (TROPICAL AIR). When the cold air and warm air meet there is rain. This meeting place is called a front. Many fronts cross Britain each year — usually moving from west to east.

The weather changes from day to day. People in Britain often say it is unpredictable but this is not really accurate. For one thing the weather experts provide forecasts which are usually fairly accurate. The weather is also predictable in that we know from past experience what the temperatures are likely to be in say July or January. This is what a weather expert means when he or she talks about 'normal temperatures for this time of year'.

The symbols at the top of the opposite page are used by weather forecasters on British television. They are used to indicate the weather expected within the next twenty-four hours.

Look at the table of symbols and then work out what the symbols represent on this weather map. Describe the weather forecast for the next day in (a) Scotland (b) South-Eastern England.

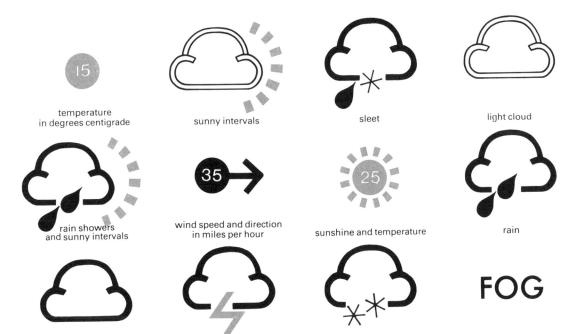

15 temperature in degrees centigrade

sunny intervals

sleet

light cloud

rain showers and sunny intervals

35 → wind speed and direction in miles per hour

25 sunshine and temperature

rain

thick clouds – overcast

thunderstorm

snow

FOG

Temperature

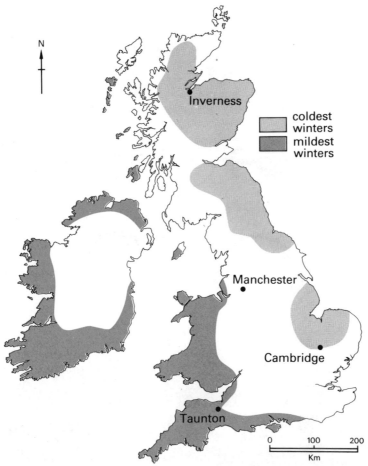

coldest winters
mildest winters

Inverness

Manchester

Cambridge

Taunton

0   100   200
Km

Although Britain is small there is a difference between mild winters in the west of the country and colder winters in the east.
In parts of Cornwall, western Wales and Scotland palm trees are able to grow. In the east they would normally be destroyed by frost. In the east the land is colder because it is closer to the cold north and east winds blowing from the North Sea.

Not all places in the west get mild winters, however. Temperatures get lower the higher up you go. It is usually about 1° Celsius colder for every 150 metres of height. This means, that although it may be warm near the sea, it is colder on the mountains. When it rains at sea level it can be snowing on the mountains.

Temperature is measured by a thermometer in degrees Celsius (or Centigrade). It is usually coldest at night (often just before dawn). It is at its warmest normally in the early afternoon. Temperatures differ like this during the day and also from day to day. If we want to know the coldest (minimum) temperature during the day a special thermometer can be used to record it. This is the maximum and minimum thermometer. It also records the highest (maximum) temperature as well.

The average temperature is halfway between the maximum and minimum temperatures. So if the maximum temperature is 15°C and the minimum temperature is 5°C the average is halfway – 10°C.

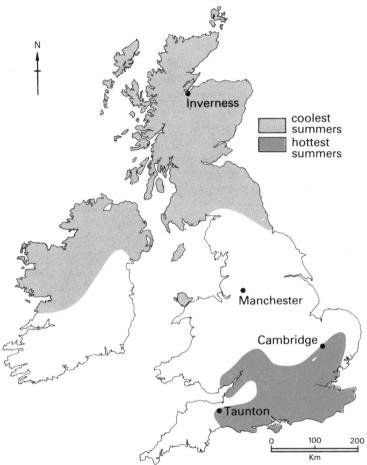

coolest summers

hottest summers

The average temperatures for every day can be added up each month and divided by the days in the month to find the average monthly temperature. If this is done for forty years and then these average temperatures are added together and divided by forty we get a good idea of the sort of temperature to expect on average in a place.

The maps on these pages show the average temperatures in Britain in January and July. These are for places which are at sea level. Mountain areas are in the coldest parts of the country at every time of the year.

As you can see in summer the temperatures get higher the nearer you get to the Equator.

In winter the temperatures get lower the further you are away from the west coast. The reason for this is because the mild weather in winter comes mainly from the Atlantic. The cold weather comes mainly from the North Sea.

One interesting thing is that only a small area has the best winters and the best summers.

Look at the two maps.
Which town is in the warmest part of the country in both winter and summer? Which town is in the areas with the coldest winters and summers? Which town has warm summers and cold winters?

49

Rainfall

The amount of rain which falls each year in Britain differs from year to year and from place to place. One year may be dry and the next year wet. Many parts of East Anglia get less than a quarter of the rain which falls on parts of the Lake District.

Rainfall is measured in millimetres. It is the depth of the rainfall which is recorded. If a bucket was left outside you could measure the rain which fell each day. The only trouble is that some of the water would evaporate. This means that it would dry up and the level in the bucket would be lower than it should be. This is why those who measure rainfall properly make sure that the rain is collected in a can with a lid on it.

If all the rain which fell from January 1st into a tank could be collected without it drying up, the depth of water on December 31st could be measured to say how much rain had fallen during the year. In parts of East Anglia the tank might be only 500 mm deep (half a metre). In parts of the Lake District it might be 3000 mm deep (three metres). This is because the Lake District is hilly and it is in the west. East Anglia is lowland and it is in the east.

Rain falls because water is taken into the air and forms clouds which bring rain. If a wet bathing costume is hung on a clothes line in hot weather it dries. The water which was in the bathing costume escapes into the air (it evaporates). It is still there even though you cannot see it. This water vapour as it is called rises into the air and as it cools forms small drops of water which collect to form clouds. Fog is very low cloud.

When the clouds get colder the drops fall as rain or as snow. They get colder when they rise higher in the air. You will remember that temperatures get lower the higher up you go. Sometimes the clouds rise because there are hills or mountains in the way. As they blow over the mountains it pours with rain. Sometimes the clouds rise because some warmer air meets colder air. Because it is warmer the air rises above the colder air and as it cools rain falls. This meeting of warm air with cold air is called a warm front, and forms part of a depression. You often hear weather forecasters talking about depressions and fronts.

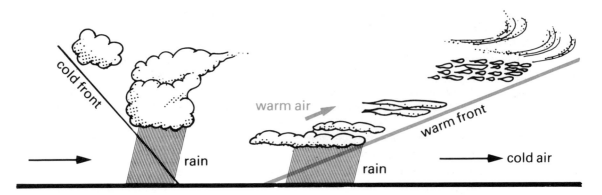

wedge of cold air forcing its way under warm air

warm air rising above cold air

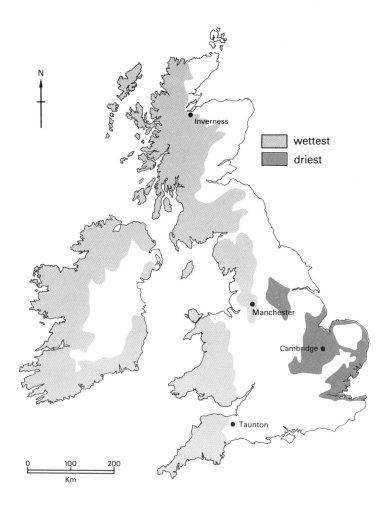

These depressions often come to Britain across the Atlantic Ocean and contain a lot of moisture. The first part of Britain they reach is the west, where most of the hills and mountains are situated. This helps to explain why the western half of Britain is generally wetter than the eastern half. The eastern counties are mainly lowland and when the depressions reach them the clouds have already lost much of their moisture. You can see these wetter and drier areas on the map on this page.

Look at the map.

Which town is in the driest area?
Write a few sentences to describe how rainfall differs from west to east in Britain.

Wind, fog and sun

In the past people used the wind to turn the sails of a windmill. It could be used for grinding corn or pumping water. The trouble with using the wind for power is that its speed is always changing. There are days when hurricanes blow and slates are ripped from the roof tops. Other days are calm and still. The strongest winds are usually at sea and at places on the coast.

This is how some of the different winds can be recognised:

if smoke from a chimney rises straight up – it is CALM

if you can feel the wind on your face – it is a LIGHT BREEZE

if dust and bits of paper are picked up by the wind – it is a BREEZE

if the telegraph wires whistle in the wind – it is a STRONG BREEZE

if it is hard to walk against the wind – it is a GALE

The direction of the wind is always the point of the compass from which it is blowing. You can find the direction of the wind by wetting your finger and holding it in the air. The side which feels the cold first of all is facing directly into the wind.

Visibility is the word used to describe how far you can see. It is said to be good when you can see a long way. When you can only see a short distance it is foggy. The different names such as THICK FOG and POOR VISIBILITY which you may hear on a weather forecast say how far you can see.

if you can see something over 10 kilometres distant – this is GOOD VISIBILITY

if the furthest you can see is less than 4 kilometres – this is POOR VISIBILITY

if you can see less than 1 kilometre – this is FOG

if you can see less than 200 metres – this is THICK FOG

if you can see less than 40 metres – this is DENSE FOG

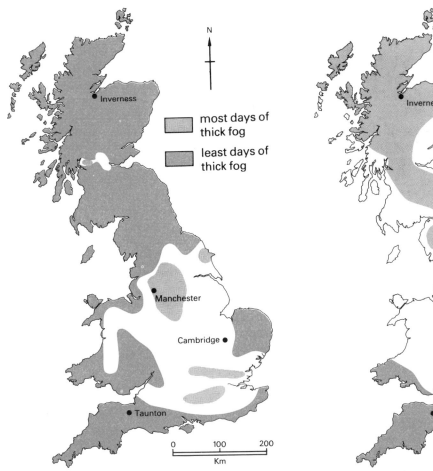

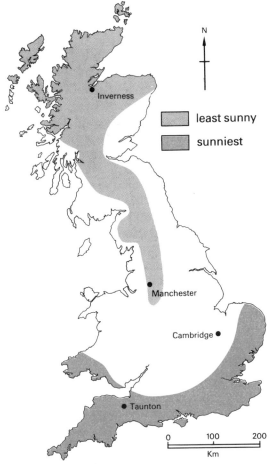

This map shows the foggiest places in Great Britain. As you can see it is chiefly the area away from the sea in England. This is because sea breezes at the coast blow away much of the mist that forms there. The area inland is also a place where lots of factories and towns send smoke and fumes into the air and these help to make the fog worse.

The sunniest places in Great Britain are the seaside resorts on the south and south-east coasts. Sunshine is measured by the number of hours of sun. The sunniest places have about 1800 hours of sun every year but in some industrial areas the hours of sun can be no more than half this amount.

Look at the maps of fog and sun.

Which is the foggiest town?

Which are the sunniest towns?

Which town do you think will have the highest number of windy days?

53

Climates of Britain

From all the weather maps on pages 48-53 you can see that there is no place in Britain which can say it has the best of every type of weather. Although the south-west is mild in winter it gets more rain than the east. Some parts of southern England are hot in summer but foggier than the rest of the country.

These different types of weather go together to make up the climate of an area. Climate describes the weather we normally expect at a place over a long period of time. The climate of London is different from the climate of the Isle of Skye in Scotland. It is wetter in Skye and much hotter in London in summer. But this does not mean that it never rains in July in London or that it is never hot enough to sun-bathe in Skye. What it does mean is that people in London can usually expect to enjoy hotter summers and a drier climate than if they lived on the Isle of Skye.

The climate of an area affects the livelihood of many outdoor workers such as farmers. In one summer in twenty the weather may turn out to be suitable for growing excellent yields of crops which are normally grown only in hotter lands (such as maize and grapes for wine). But farmers usually stick to the crops they expect to grow well in an average summer unless their land is specially favoured. Occasionally a harvest fails because the weather is well below average. In Britain the climate of East Anglia (which has warmer and sunnier summers and is dry all the year round) is better suited to growing crops than the climate of south-western Ireland (which is wet all the year round). However in south-western Ireland the farmers can rear livestock out of doors all the year round because the winters are mild. In East Anglia livestock farmers have to bring cows and fat cattle indoors in the winter months to shelter them from the cold.

Trace the outline of the map of Britain below. Mark on your tracing the position of your home town or village (or select a town or village where a relative lives).

Look in turn at each of the maps on pages 48–53.

Is your town or village in any of the shaded areas on these maps? The colour indicates the areas which get the best of the weather and the grey areas show the parts of the country which get the worst of the weather.

Place the tracing paper over each map and if the dot marking your town or village falls within the shaded area find out what this shading means.

Make a list of the things you discover about the climate of your town or village. For instance when you place tracing paper over the map on page 48 write down MILD WINTERS if the dot falls within the coloured area. Write COLD WINTERS if it falls within the grey area.

Do the same for summers (HOT SUMMERS and COOL SUMMERS), rainfall (WET and DRY), fog (FOGGIEST and LEAST FOGGY) and sun (SUNNIEST and DULLEST).

Do any parts of Britain fall within the coloured area on every map?

Do any parts of Britain fall within the grey area on every map?

Which parts of Britain do you think have the best climate?

N

0   100   200
Km

Exercises

1. Look at each of these statements. Decide which are TRUE and which are FALSE. If the statement is true write TRUE and copy the statement out as it stands. If the statement is false write FALSE and then correct the statement and write it out accurately.
   (a) It usually gets colder the higher up you go.
   (b) Rainfall in Britain is higher in the east than in the west.
   (c) Hilly areas in Britain are almost always wetter than the nearby lowlands.
   (d) In Britain the east is not as cold as the west in winter.
   (e) In Britain the south is warmer than the north in summer.
   (f) The foggiest parts of Britain are at the coast.
   (g) The sunniest places in Britain are on the west coast.
   (h) The meeting of warm air with cold air is called a front.

2. Look at these temperature statistics for London for a period of ten days in June.
   MAXIMUM TEMPERATURE 18 16 17 18 23 25 29 31 20 26
   MINIMUM TEMPERATURE 12 12 6 8 5 10 10 12 12 10
   (a) What is the maximum temperature recorded for this period of ten days?
   (b) What is the lowest temperature recorded during this period of ten days?

3. Complete these sentences
   (a) Dense fog is when you can see ....
   (b) If you can see something over 10km distant this is ....
   (c) A gale is when ....

4. Look at this weather map. Describe the weather expected in (a) south-west England (b) northern Ireland (c) northern Scotland.

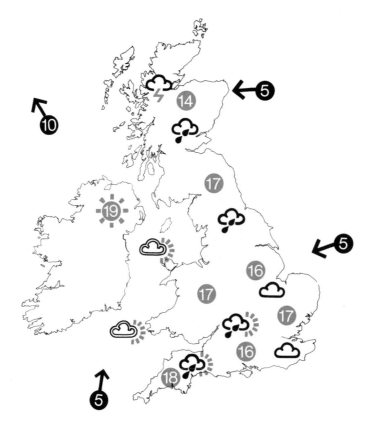

FARMING

From an aeroplane the British Isles appear as a mass of green fields and mountain pastures. Unfortunately the amount of new building around the towns grows every year. The land taken for building plots and for motorways is usually land which produces crops or is used for grazing animals. These are the two types of farming.

Generally speaking crops grow better where the weather is hot, dry and sunny — particularly in the eastern counties of England. Animals do better on the rich grasslands of the west country. This is because the heavier rainfall and milder winters help the grass to grow.

Most farmers grow some crops. This is called arable farming. Most farmers also grow grass and keep some animals. This is called livestock farming. The two types of farming are not kept separate from each other on a farm. The crops provide some of the food for the animals and the manure from the cowsheds and piggeries is used to feed the soils to get better crops. Farms which have both arable farming and livestock farming are often called mixed farms.

Crops are grown both for food for people and for livestock. Food for animals is called fodder. The main types of crop grown in Britain are shown in this box:

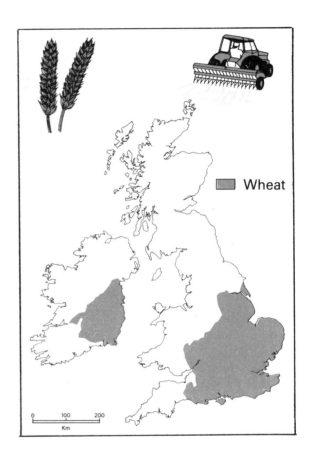

Wheat

CEREALS	Wheat Oats Barley	OTHERS Flowers
ROOTS	Potatoes Sugar Beet Turnips	Vegetables (such as peas)
GRASS	for silage for hay	Orchard fruits (such as apples) Soft fruits (such as strawberries)

Arable farming

The maps below and on page 57 show the main areas where cereal crops are grown in Britain.

Corn crops, such as wheat and barley, need summer sun and heat to ripen. They grow best in rich soils. It helps if the land is flat or level and if the fields are large. This is so that large tractors and combine harvesters can be used without having to turn round frequently to go back up another row. In parts of East Anglia many hedges have been uprooted and flattened to make the fields even bigger.

Cereals, such as wheat and barley, grow ears of corn and these are ground in a mill. They are used to make flour (from wheat), malted to make beer (barley) and used to feed livestock. Some foods are made from other cereals such as porridge from oats, ryebread from rye and cornflakes from maize. Britain does not grow enough cereals for the needs of the people living there and wheat, maize, rice and other cereals are imported (brought into the country from abroad).

Copy the outline of the map on page 57. Show on it the main areas of wheat with one series of coloured dots. Use another colour to show barley.

Mark with a dot the position of your home town or village (or that of a town or village where a relative lives). Is that town or village situated in or near an area noted for its corn growing?

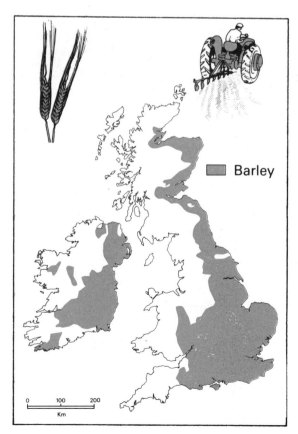

Barley

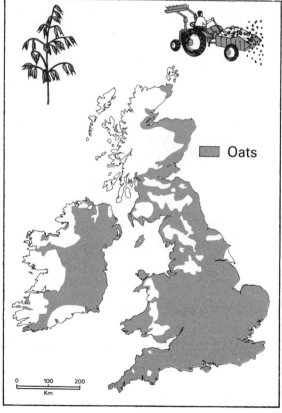

Oats

Root crops provide food for people (potatoes) and for livestock (turnips). Sugar beet is made into sugar whilst the leftover parts of the beet are fed to livestock. Nowadays machines harvest many root crops. In the past potatoes were picked by hand, now a machine can do the job.

Potatoes and sugar beet grow best on the same sort of land as wheat and barley. For sugar beet the farmer has to make an arrangement with a sugar beet factory to take his or her crop. Even if a farmer in another district wanted to grow sugar beet there would be no point in doing so if there were no sugar beet factories nearby.

Look at the five maps on pages 57—59.

1. Which are the most important crop growing areas in the British Isles?

2. Turn back to the weather maps on pages 48–53 and to the map of hills on page 23 and see if you can think of two or three reasons why these are the most important crop growing areas in Britain.

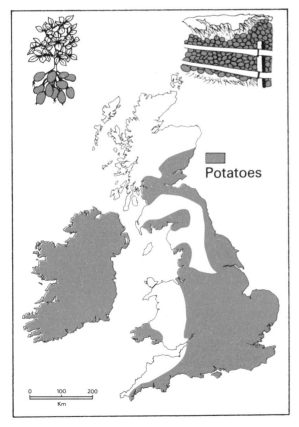

Potatoes

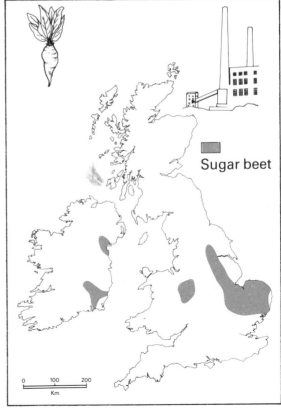

Sugar beet

Market gardening

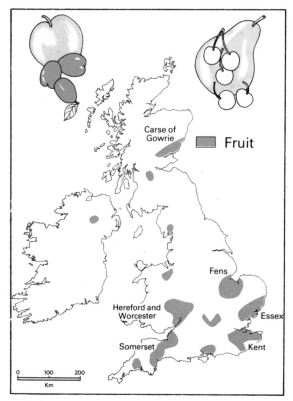

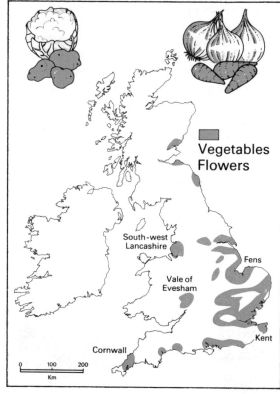

Many farms specialise in growing crops which need a lot of attention but which can be sold for high prices. Sometimes they are grown on large farms but often they are grown on small-holdings (small farms) and often in glass-houses. This type of farming is sometimes called market-gardening because the produce will be sold at a market. Nowadays this is not always strictly true. Many farmers grow vegetables like peas and beans for a local canning factory or for a frozen foods firm. Many farmers grow fruit such as strawberries for a jam factory or apples for a cider company.

Fruits like strawberries and gooseberries are called soft fruits to distinguish them from orchard fruits such as apples and pears.

The maps on this page show the chief areas of Britain noted for their market-gardening produce. Some of these areas are specially noted for particular crops such as hops (for beer) in Kent, apples (for cider) in Hereford-shire and Somerset, spring flowers from Corn-wall and the Scilly Isles, strawberries from the Fens and rhubarb from the West Yorkshire area south of Leeds.

Vegetables, fruits and flowers can be dam-aged by frosts. Since frost is often more com-mon at the bottom of a slope and deep in a valley many fruit farms in the West Country are situated higher up on a slope, facing south (to catch the sun).

Look at the maps.

Which parts of Britain are most important for growing fruit, vegetables and flowers?

Look at the weather maps on pages 48–53 and at the towns map on page 123.

What reasons help to explain why these areas are noted for market-gardening?

Grass

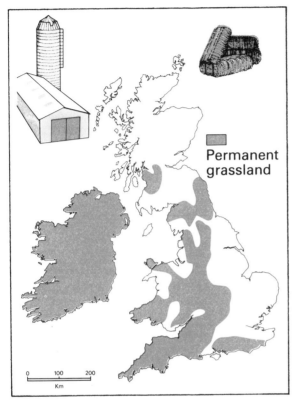

Permanent grassland

0   100   200
Km

Grasses are grown either as a crop for one or two years or in a field of permanent grassland (meaning that it is always grass). Fields like these are often called meadows. The grass can be cut to make hay or cut to make silage. The old square haystacks are disappearing in some parts of the country where farmers use harvesters which bind the hay into round bales. Grass cut for silage is chopped up and blown into a trailer using a machine called a forage harvester. It is then stored in a pit or a tower until it is ready to be eaten by livestock. The smell of silage is sometimes unpleasant.

The things which crops need in order to grow are shown in the picture.

Crops need

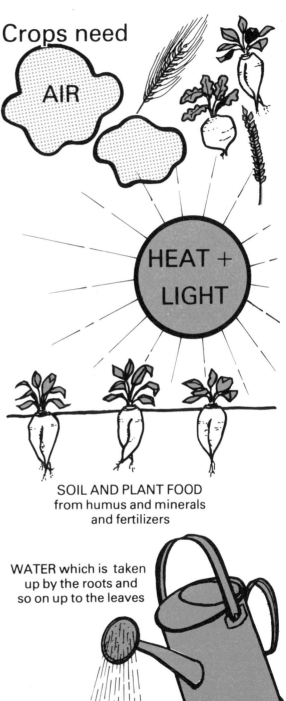

AIR

HEAT + LIGHT

SOIL AND PLANT FOOD
from humus and minerals
and fertilizers

WATER which is taken
up by the roots and
so on up to the leaves

The farmer's year

Before the crops are sown the land has to be prepared by ploughing, harrowing, discing and rolling. This is to turn over the soil and break up the large clods of soil. When the soil is fine and crumbly the corn seed is sown in drills (rows) using a seed drill pulled by a tractor.

Corn crops may have to be sprayed during the growing season against pests and weeds. Root crops need more attention. Turnips have to be singled so that the plants have plenty of room in which to grow. Potatoes are ridged up with banks of soil.

In June or July the grass is ready for harvest (hay-making or silage) and in July, August and September the corn crops are ready for combining. A combine harvester can cut the corn and thrash (beat) it so that the ears of corn separate from the stalks (straw). The corn is collected in sacks or pours from a pipe into a trailer travelling alongside. The straw is later baled (a machine packs it into large bricks of straw), or if straw is plentiful and not wanted on the farm, it is burnt in the fields. The ash makes good fertiliser.

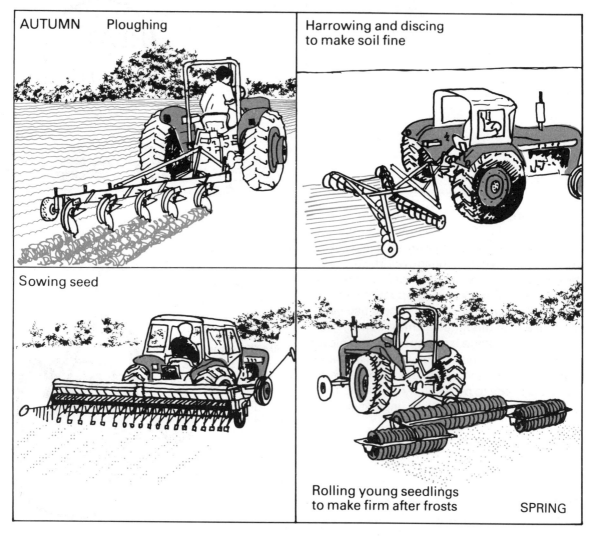

AUTUMN   Ploughing

Harrowing and discing to make soil fine

Sowing seed

Rolling young seedlings to make firm after frosts   SPRING

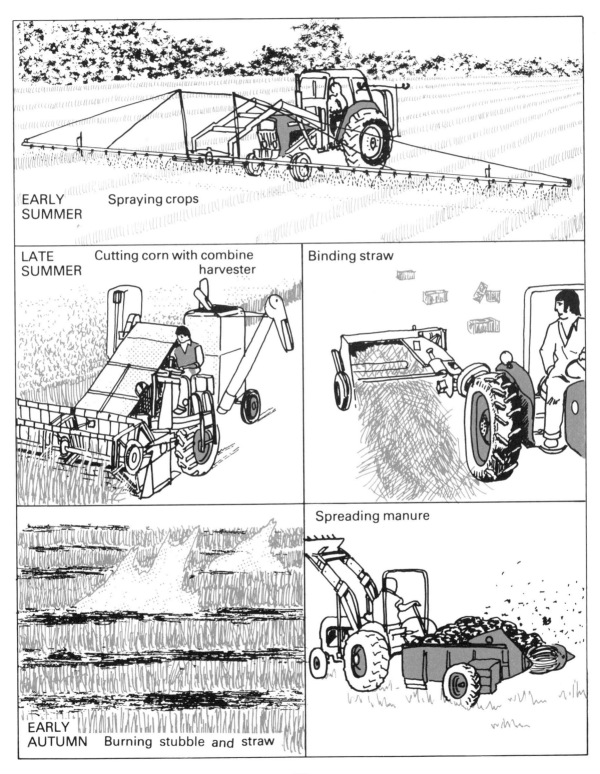

EARLY SUMMER   Spraying crops

LATE SUMMER   Cutting corn with combine harvester

Binding straw

EARLY AUTUMN   Burning stubble and straw

Spreading manure

Keeping livestock

Although crops are very important in Britain they only cover one-third of the total land used for farming. The other two-thirds are used for grazing animals. Livestock farming and pastoral farming are other names for this type of farming. Slightly more than half of the grassland is rough grazing. This is the name for mountain and hill pastures which are left as they are. The higher parts are grazed almost entirely by sheep. The meadowlands are used chiefly for grazing cattle.

The diagram on this page shows what animals need.

Look at it and then at the picture on page 61 showing what crops need.

Write down which needs of animals are (a) the same as those for growing crops (b) different from those for crops.

Animals need

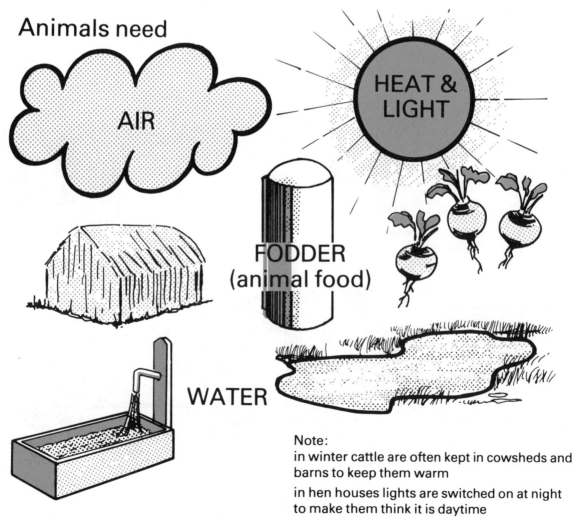

AIR

HEAT & LIGHT

FODDER (animal food)

WATER

Note:
in winter cattle are often kept in cowsheds and barns to keep them warm

in hen houses lights are switched on at night to make them think it is daytime

Cattle

Some farms are mainly dairy farms. This means that they keep herds of cows and make most of their money from selling milk. They may also grow crops but these are usually fodder crops for the cows in winter. Dairy cows have to be well fed if they are to produce a lot of good milk. They also have to give birth to a calf each year. Some female calves can be reared by the farmer to become cows to replace any old animals in the herd which can no longer produce good milk. But half the calves are male and many of the female calves are unsuitable for rearing as dairy cows. These animals are fattened as beef cattle. Sometimes they are fattened on the dairy farm and often they are sold when young to other farmers who make most of their money from rearing beef cattle for the butcher. Beef cattle are not as fussy as cows. A farmer can feed three beef animals on the same land which is needed for

feeding two dairy cows. Sheep need even less grazing land. That same plot of land could feed twelve sheep and lambs.

The map shows the original homes of the main cattle breeds to be seen in Britain today. The best dairy breeds give high-yields (amounts) of milk or milk which is rich and creamy. The beef breeds are those which produce the best meat and the dual-purpose breeds are those which are suitable for milk and meat production.

In the map on page 66 you can see that the most important areas for rearing cattle are in the west. Cows do best on grass. Grass grows well where there is plenty of rainfall and warmth. In Ireland, Cornwall, Devon, Somerset and round the coast of Wales the mild winters, warm summers and high rainfall make these areas ideal for grass growing.

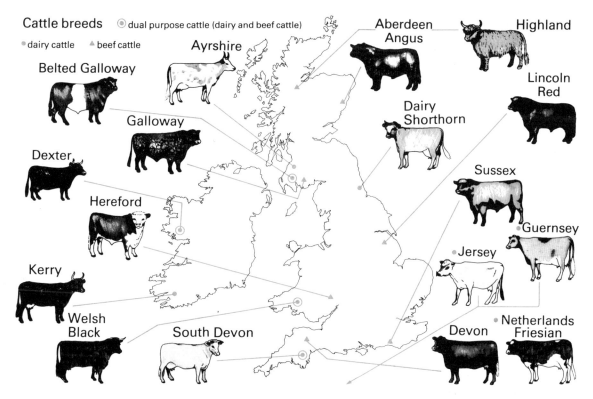

Cattle breeds   ◉ dual purpose cattle (dairy and beef cattle)
• dairy cattle   ▲ beef cattle

Belted Galloway
Ayrshire
Aberdeen Angus
Highland
Lincoln Red
Galloway
Dairy Shorthorn
Dexter
Sussex
Hereford
Guernsey
Jersey
Kerry
Welsh Black
South Devon
Devon
Netherlands Friesian

There are many dairy farms in the drier east even so. This is because the farmers close to the big industrial areas find it worthwhile to supply the local market with fresh milk. In the more remote parts of Britain it may be too costly to send the milk by lorry and train. In these areas the surplus milk is made into cheese or dried milk. In southern Ireland much of the milk is made into butter.

Look at the map below and at the map of cattle breeds on page 65.

Write two or three sentences to describe which parts of Britain are most important for cattle rearing.

Which parts of the British Isles were the original homes of (a) the dairy breeds (b) the beef breeds?

Copy the cattle rearing map and mark on it the position of your town or village (or that of a town or village where a relative lives).

Does it lie within an area which is important for cattle rearing?

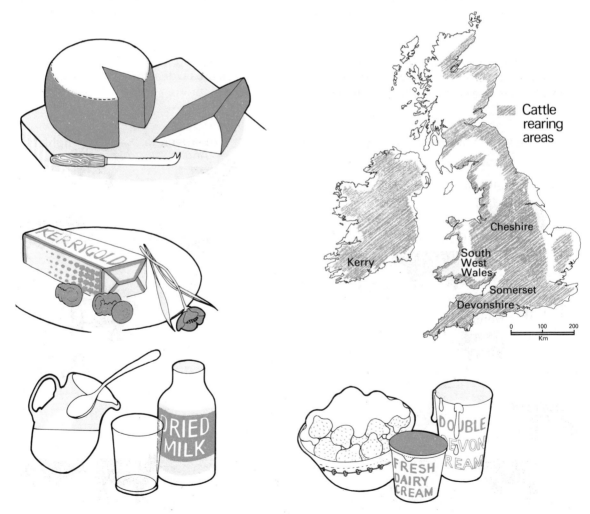

Cattle rearing areas

Cheshire
South West Wales
Kerry
Somerset
Devonshire

0   100   200
Km

A day on a dairy farm

Life on a dairy farm is often monotonous. Twice daily the cows have to be brought into the dairy or milking parlour for milking. It does not matter what day of the year it is this routine has to be performed – Christmas Day included. On a small dairy farm run by a man and wife this often means that they are never able to take holidays.

In summer the cows graze in the fields. In winter they have to be kept under shelter in most parts of Britain. Only where the weather is very mild can they be left outdoors. In summer the cows feed on grass – the best food for cows producing milk. In winter the grass does not grow except in the very mild and wet areas of the south west. Cows then feed on hay or silage or special foods prepared from corn and oil.

There are a lot of indoor jobs for the farmer in winter – taking fodder to the cows and calves, cleaning out the sheds where the cows are kept, cleaning and sterilising equipment used in the dairy.

In summer the dairy farmer is just as busy growing fodder crops such as turnips, making hay or silage, bringing the cows into the dairy twice a day.

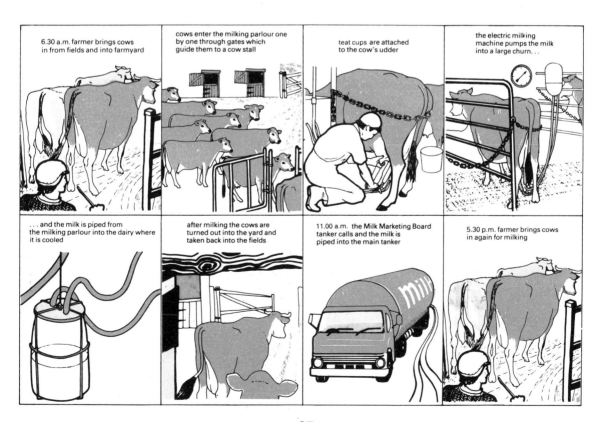

6.30 a.m. farmer brings cows in from fields and into farmyard

cows enter the milking parlour one by one through gates which guide them to a cow stall

teat cups are attached to the cow's udder

the electric milking machine pumps the milk into a large churn. . .

. . . and the milk is piped from the milking parlour into the dairy where it is cooled

after milking the cows are turned out into the yard and taken back into the fields

11.00 a.m. the Milk Marketing Board tanker calls and the milk is piped into the main tanker

5.30 p.m. farmer brings cows in again for milking

Sheep farming

The pastures are poor on the hills and usually unsuitable for most types of farming. Only a hardy animal like the sheep is able to climb the rough slopes, survive the hard winters and do well on rough grazing. The lambs born to the ewes (the female sheep) are not so hardy and they are usually taken to the lowlands to be sold to other farmers who fatten them for butcher's meat on richer lowland pastures. The ewes are called breeding ewes. The lambs they produce are the principal source of money for the hill farmer. The fleece of wool which is taken from the sheep in the summer is also important.

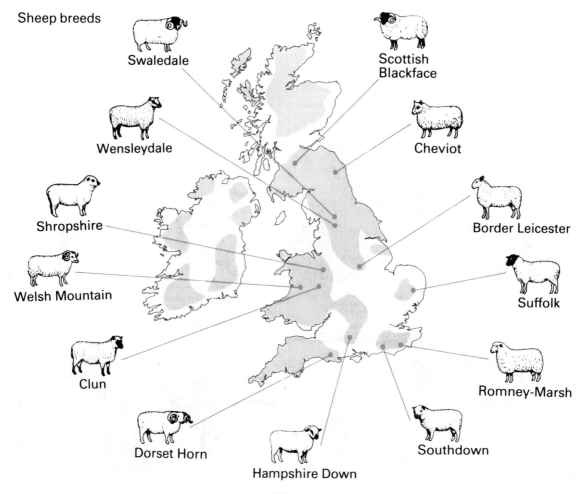

Sheep breeds

Swaledale

Scottish Blackface

Wensleydale

Cheviot

Shropshire

Border Leicester

Welsh Mountain

Suffolk

Clun

Romney-Marsh

Dorset Horn

Southdown

Hampshire Down

A year on a hill sheep farm

JANUARY—FEBRUARY
digging ewes out of snowdrifts

MARCH to APRIL   lambing season begins

MAY
motherless lambs fed from bottle

JUNE to JULY   sheep shearing

AUGUST

sheep dipping

SEPTEMBER   lambs taken from ewes .....

SEPTEMBER .... and sold as stores to be fattened on rich lowland pastures

OCTOBER to NOVEMBER   ewes mated with rams

DECEMBER   fodder taken out to sheep on hill pastures

On a hill sheep farm life varies from month to month. It does not follow the same routine as on a dairy farm.

The busiest time is lambing time in the spring. The farmer and shepherds have to be on call at all hours of day and night. A ewe in difficulties giving birth to her lambs could easily die without the help of the shepherd. Some lambs lose their mothers and the farmer then tries to get a ewe who has lost a lamb to take the lamb and feed it. To make the ewe think the other lamb is her own the dead lamb's skin is draped over the head of the lamb so that it smells the same. This saves the farmer having to spend time and money feeding the lambs by hand on bottles of cow's milk.

There are different occasions during the year when the sheep and lambs are gathered together. This is when the shepherd appreciates good sheepdogs.

Copy the sheep farming map opposite.

Mark on it the position of your home town or village (or that of a town of village where a relative lives).

How far is the town or village you have marked from an important sheep rearing area? Write out the names of the chief sheep farming areas (the map on page 23 will help you to do this).

Why do sheep farmers fear snow blizzards in March and April?

Pigs and poultry

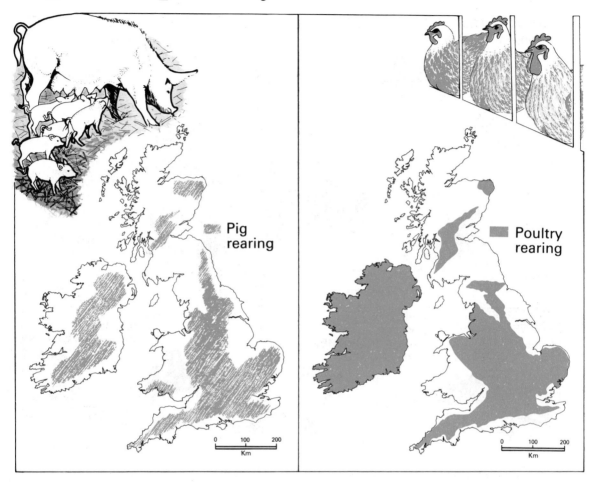

Pigs can be fattened into meat for bacon, pork, ham or sausage meat in a short time. Pig farming is usually carried on in special pig units. These piggeries are like factories. The young pigs are kept in special buildings which do not allow them much exercise. In this way they gain weight rapidly.

Poultry used to be kept by most farmers in hen houses and allowed to wander all over the farmyard searching for food. They still do on some farms and the eggs from these hens are called 'free range eggs'. Nowadays the large producers of eggs, chickens and turkeys keep their poultry in huge sheds or poultry houses where the birds are kept in warm, well-lit conditions. The food is fed to the chickens and turkeys by machines. The chickens are kept in cages and the eggs roll down from each cage into a trough for ease of collection. The poultry houses, like the piggeries, are sometimes said to be factory farms.

Is the type of weather likely to have any effect on whether a farmer keeps pigs or poultry? Give a reason for your answer.

Why is this type of farming called 'factory farming'?

Look at the maps. Which parts of the British Isles are most important for pigs and poultry?

Farming today

Although farming in Britain provides jobs for only two or three people in every hundred it is one of the most important industries. The crops and animal produce grown on British farms help to provide much of the food needed in Britain.

British farming is one of the most efficient systems of farming in the world. It is said to be one of the most highly mechanised. This means that many more machines are used on British farms than is the case with some other farming countries.

In the last twenty years British farmers have increased the amount of food produced by half as much again. They have used new methods such as fertilisers and crop sprays to increase the amount of wheat and barley.

As you have already seen some soils are better than others for crops. The reason they are better is because they may be easier to dig or to plough, may be less likely to become waterlogged and may contain plenty of food for the plants. This is where the farmer can make improvements. Drainpipes can help to drain the land whilst manures, fertilisers, lime and peat can help to improve different types of soil. At the same time crop sprays can help to kill pests and prevent diseases. Water can be provided in dry areas by irrigation from pipes rather than by relying on rainfall.

The increase in the amount of food produced has not just been in crops. British cows now produce more milk, hens produce more eggs and efficient pig farming has meant more bacon as well.

Despite the efficiency of British farming, we still have to buy a lot of food from other countries.
Look in the kitchen at home and make a list of any foods which have come from other countries. Note down also the countries they come from.

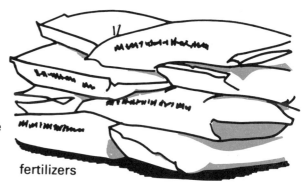

fertilizers

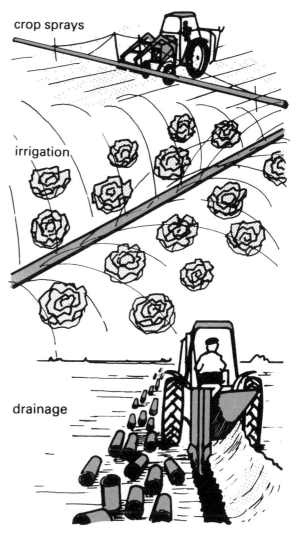

crop sprays

irrigation

drainage

Some of the things which a farmer takes into account when planning any changes in the way the land is farmed are shown in the picture on this page. Usually a change is only made if there are very good reasons for the change. This is because the farm usually has buildings which are suited for particular types of farming. If a dairy farmer decides to change he or she may have to scrap a dairy fitted with expensive machinery and equipment. If the farmer decides not to make silage in future it may be a problem knowing what to do with the tall silage towers on the farm.

The arable farm is usually equipped with expensive machines and implements for producing crops.

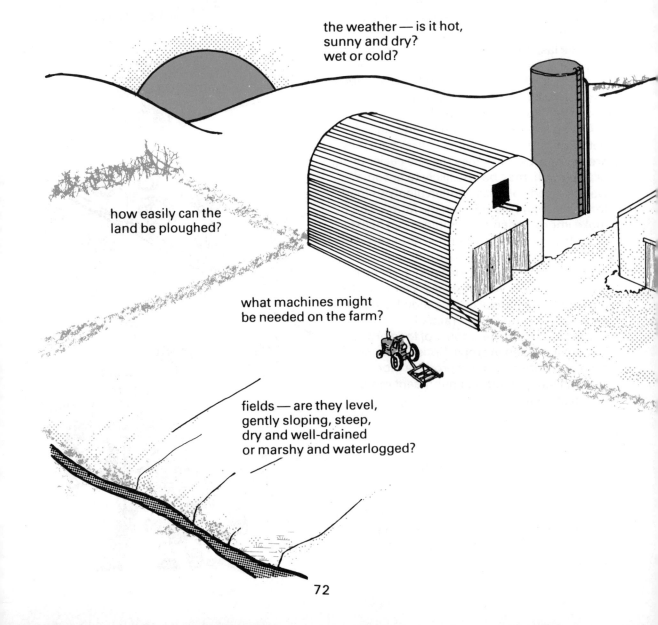

the weather — is it hot, sunny and dry? wet or cold?

how easily can the land be ploughed?

what machines might be needed on the farm?

fields — are they level, gently sloping, steep, dry and well-drained or marshy and waterlogged?

The farmer who wants to grow wheat and barley on a large scale has to spend a lot of money on machines like combine harvesters and on machinery to dry the grain when it is harvested.

For these reasons changes on a farm are usually made gradually. But changes are made. If too many crops are grown the prices may be low and if the farmer does not receive enough money from selling farm produce to pay the workers or pay for the seed there may be a need to choose some other type of farming. But if every farmer changed there would soon be a shortage of that crop. This is one reason why farmers often get payments from the government to help keep the prices of farm produce from falling or rising suddenly.

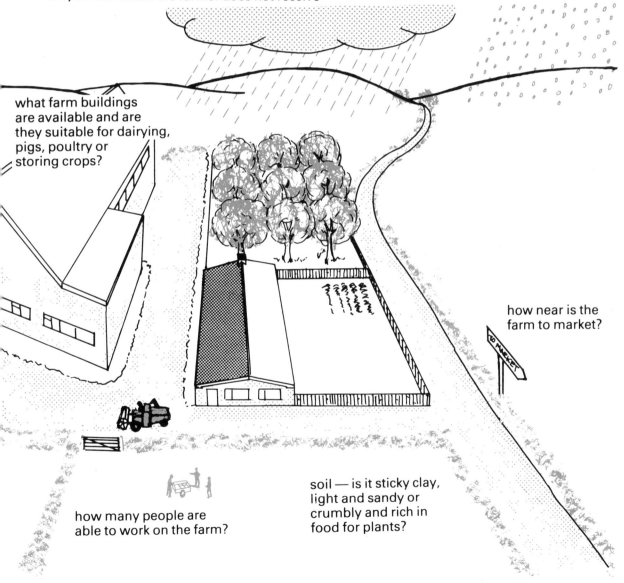

what farm buildings are available and are they suitable for dairying, pigs, poultry or storing crops?

how near is the farm to market?

how many people are able to work on the farm?

soil — is it sticky clay, light and sandy or crumbly and rich in food for plants?

Exercises

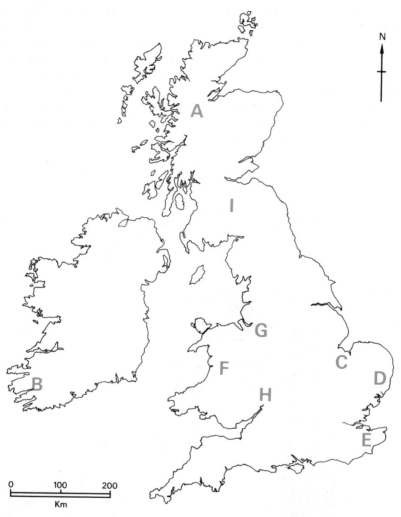

Look at the map.

1. What type of farming would you expect to see in the areas marked A, B, C, D, E, F, G, H, I?

2. Give two reasons for each of the types of farming to be seen at A, B, C.

3. Complete the following sentences
   Pastoral farming is ....
   Rough grazing is ....
   Arable farming is ....
   Farms which have both arable farming and livestock are called ....farms.

Food for animals is called ....
Wheat, barley and oats are c......n crops – sometimes known as c......l crops.
Farms growing vegetables and fruit are often called m......t g......s.
Very small farms are often called ....

4. What machines (a) harvest corn (b) cut grass for silage (c) sow corn?

5. Name three things needed (a) by crops (b) by animals.

6. Look at the picture of the farm.
Trace or copy this outline.
Write down the answers to these questions.
(a) Which part of the farm is likely to be wet underfoot long after the other fields are dry?
(b) Where do you think the farmer would get materials for the fences on the farm?
(c) Is the farm level or sloping?
(d) Where would you keep a flock of sheep on this farm?

(e) Dairy cows have to be milked twice a day in the dairy on the farm. In which field would you graze the cows in summer to save a long walk with the herd twice daily? Where would you keep other cattle?
(f) Which fields might be suitable for growing crops?

Print CROPS, COWS, SHEEP, CATTLE over the fields you have chosen on your copy of this picture.

75

INDUSTRY

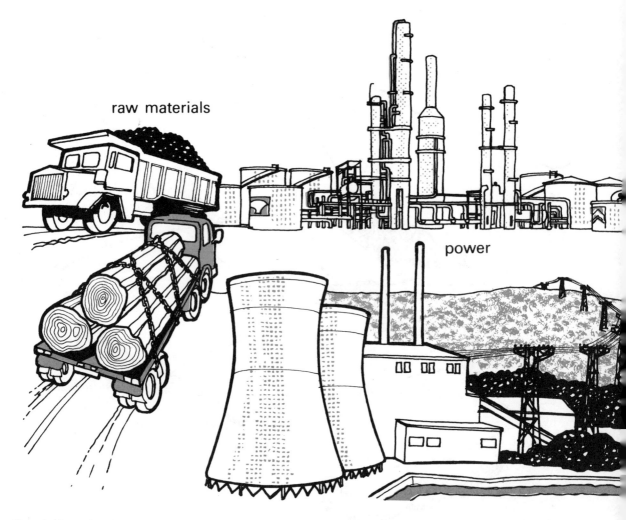

raw materials

power

Britain lives by the things she makes in factories and in works. There is not enough farmland to provide food to feed all the fifty million people who live in Britain nor is there an adequate supply of all the raw materials needed. Raw materials are the things from which other goods can be made. For instance iron ore is earth which contains iron, paper is made from trees and nylon comes from coal.

To make something you always need raw materials. You usually need some form of power as well unless it is to be made by hand alone. Modern sources of power are coal, electricity, gas and oil. In the past power came from windmills, watermills and horses. You also need labour — people to work the machines. Very up-to-date factories have machines which are as automatic as possible, not needing workers to operate (work) them. Even so some people are needed to see that the automatic machines are working properly.

Lastly the products (the things that are produced) which have been manufactured (made) have to be packed, taken away and sold to customers. The customers may be other factories, shops or businesses and sometimes the goods may be sold to customers who order the goods by letter. The word market is used to describe the places where the goods are sold

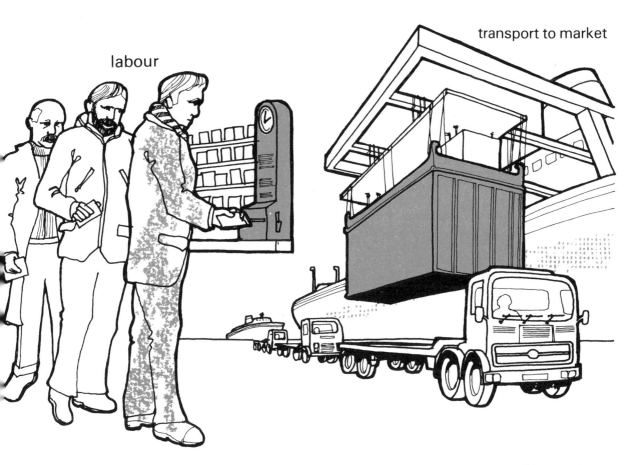

labour

transport to market

and the people who buy them. A brewery supplying beer to the local public houses can be said to be situated close to its market.

Sometimes other products are produced as well as the main product. These are called by-products. In a woollen mill raw wool is cleaned. The manufacturers remove lanolin oil from the wool but instead of throwing it away they sell it for use in making soap and beauty preparations.

There are also waste products which are of no value and these have to be got rid of. Some-times if there are many waste products the manufacturer has a problem knowing what to do with them. In some industrial areas the waste products of the past were just tipped on to waste ground to make small hills (slag heaps) which spoil the landscape. In other areas they were (and sometimes still are) poured into a river and washed away into the sea.

These waste products can spoil an area. This is called pollution. It can still be seen in many factory towns. There are blackened buildings which were caused by chimney smoke in the past. In some rivers you can see thick froth, oil, sludge and coloured water from dyes and chemicals.

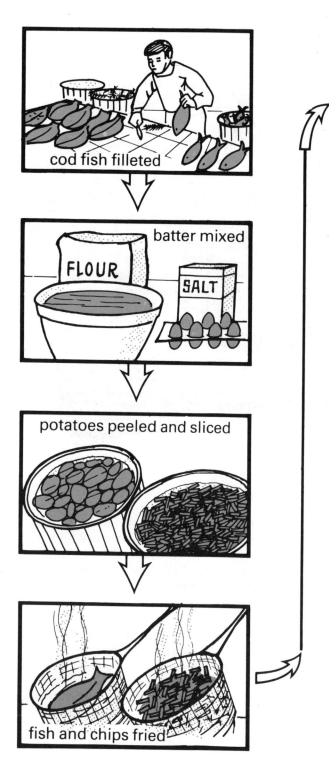

cod fish filleted

batter mixed

FLOUR
SALT

potatoes peeled and sliced

fish and chips fried

fish wrapped in paper

fish and chips sold to customers

potato peelings put in a bin for the pigs

eggshells, fish bones and skin and waste paper thrown into dustbin

In the pictures on page 78 you can see that a fish and chip shop is like a small factory.

It needs *raw materials* – fish, potatoes and the ingredients to make batter. It needs a source of *power* – electricity for the fat fryer. It needs *labour* – the people who run the shop. The raw materials have to be manufactured into fish and chips. This means a number of different jobs which have to be done in the right order. It would be silly to slice the potatoes before peeling them! This is called a *production line* in a factory and the jobs which turn raw materials into a finished product are said to *process* them.

The fish and chips are the *main product* Since the potato peelings can be used to feed pigs this is a *by-product,* it is not thrown away. The *waste products* which have to be thrown away include egg shells, empty containers which cannot be used again and the dirty water from the basin used for washing the potatoes.

Wherever possible manufacturers try to re-use raw materials which are necessary on the production line. This is called re-cycling them. A steel works uses scraps of steel which are discarded (not used) in one process and puts them back in the furnace to make new steel. In the fish and chip shop the cooking oil is used again and the milk bottles are returned to the dairy.

Copy the diagram below

Write in the boxes which have been left empty the names of the raw materials, labour, power, processes, main products, by-products and waste products when making fish and chips.

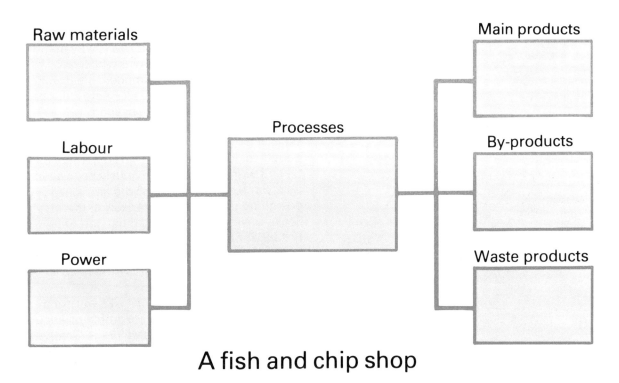

Raw materials

Labour

Power

Processes

Main products

By-products

Waste products

A fish and chip shop

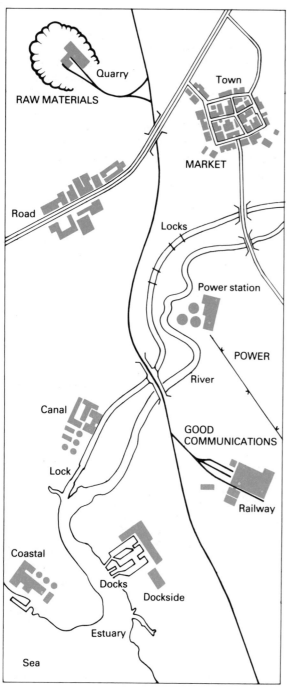

The diagram on page 92 shows some of the raw materials and sources of power used in a big iron and steel works. Although this works has many buildings and occupies a huge site and employs thousands of workers it is very similar to the fish and chip shop.

Manufacturers try to produce their goods as cheaply as possible. It may be costly to take fuel or heavy raw materials a long way by lorry or train. So they may have to build their factories near the raw materials or near a source of power such as a coal mine or a power station.

It may be even more expensive to take the finished products to the customers – especially if they are very heavy or bulky or if they are fragile or will not keep more than a day or two. There may be a need then to build the factory close to the market – the place where the goods will be sold.

Sometimes a good place for a factory is somewhere in the middle or where there are good roads, railways or docks. It may be a very convenient place to bring in raw materials and take out finished products. This is why many factories are situated in towns which have good roads. It is also why modern steel works are often situated at the coast where ships can bring the iron ore and coke needed.

Factories often need workers with particular skills. It might cost too much to have to train people to do a special job in an area where this type of work has never previously been available. For example workers who are skilled in designing pottery are more likely to live in Stoke-on-Trent than in any other part of Britain. A firm wishing to make pottery in Britain on a large scale would think twice before building their pottery works in any other part of the country.

But there are other problems as well for a new manufacturer. There are problems about finding a suitable plot of land for the factory. Some works need a large flat plot, others need a river site, some need a railway line. All need good roads. Even if the manufacturers find the ideal site they still have to get permission to build their factory there. If their works is likely to block out a lovely view, or poison the atmosphere with smoke and fumes, or if there are too many factories in that particular area already, then they may not be allowed to go ahead with their plans.

Copy the diagram below and write out in full the words for which initial letters have been given.

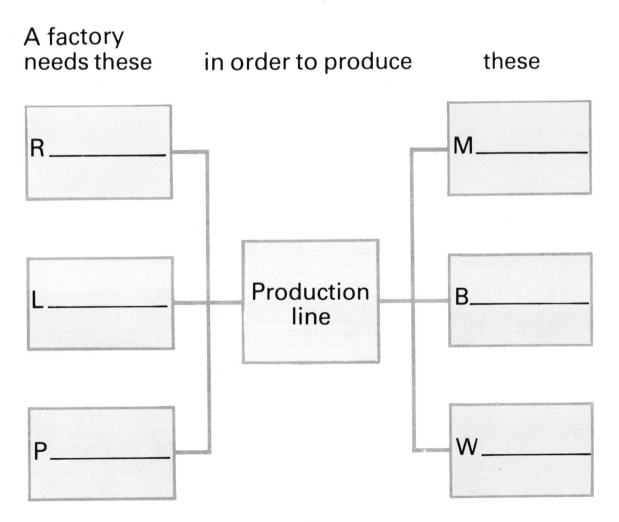

A factory needs these   in order to produce   these

R_____

L_____

P_____

Production line

M_____

B_____

W_____

Power for industry

The main sources of power for industry in Britain (and for use in private homes) are coal, electricity, oil and gas. Electricity can be produced by burning coal, oil or gas and from running water (called hydro-electricity) or from nuclear energy.

Coal-burning power stations produce most of the electricity. Fifty years ago coal was easily the most important source of power. It was used to provide the fuel for steam engines in trains, ships and factories. The drawback was that it was dirty to handle, it filled the air with smoke and it was heavy to move over long distances.

Each fuel has advantages and disadvantages like this. Electricity is the cleanest fuel but it is often more expensive than the other fuels. One of its advantages, like gas but unlike coal and oil, is that it is not stored at the factory.

This diagram shows what happens at a power station.

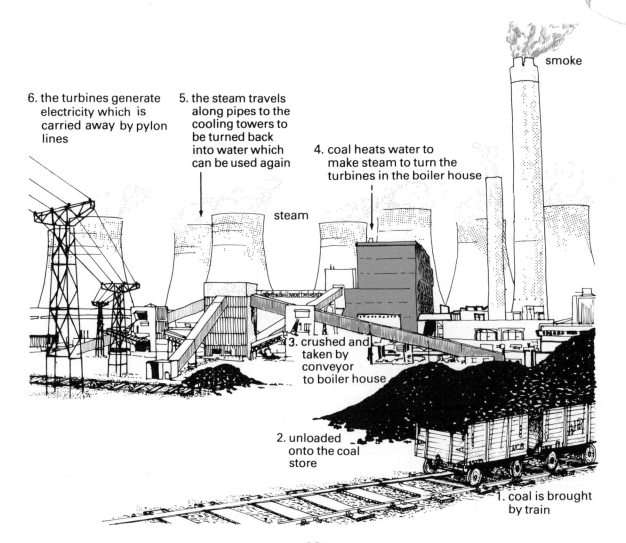

smoke

6. the turbines generate electricity which is carried away by pylon lines

5. the steam travels along pipes to the cooling towers to be turned back into water which can be used again

steam

4. coal heats water to make steam to turn the turbines in the boiler house

3. crushed and taken by conveyor to boiler house

2. unloaded onto the coal store

1. coal is brought by train

The best place for a power station burning coal is on a coalfield. In the photograph below you can see the Lea Hall Colliery and the Rugeley Power Station in Staffordshire.

Write down the advantages of building a power station here.

At Kellingley Colliery in Yorkshire railway trucks which never stop fill up with coal and deliver it (again without ever stopping) to Drax Power Station.

Some electricity in Britain is produced from water-power and some from nuclear energy.

Hydro-electricity is produced when water is made to fall from a height and forces a turbine round at high speed as if it were a water wheel. The only places where hydro-electricity can be produced cheaply are in the mountains. Most of the hydro-electric power stations in Britain are in Scotland and in Wales. You can see where the main stations are situated in the map on the opposite page.

Nuclear energy (or atomic power as it is sometimes called) can also be used. It works like coal by providing heat to make steam. Nuclear power stations like the one shown in the photograph are almost always situated at the coast as you can see in the map opposite.

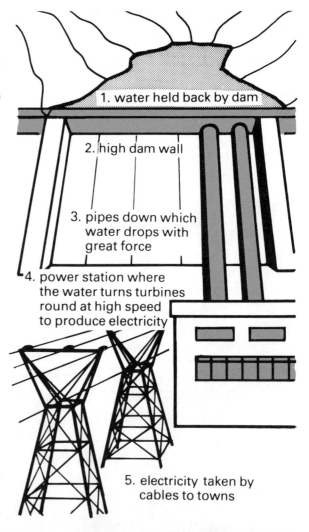

1. water held back by dam

2. high dam wall

3. pipes down which water drops with great force

4. power station where the water turns turbines round at high speed to produce electricity

5. electricity taken by cables to towns

Hunterston nuclear power station

Coal

The main coalfields in Great Britain are shown in this map. The dots indicate some of the biggest coal-burning power stations, the squares indicate nuclear power stations and the letter H indicates areas where there are several hydro-electric power stations.

Look at the map.

Which parts of Britain are noted for (a) coal mining (b) coal-burning power stations (c) hydro-electric power stations (d) nuclear power stations?

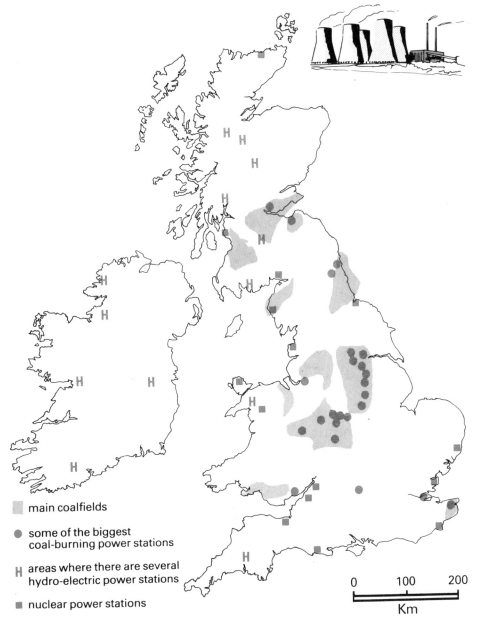

■ main coalfields

● some of the biggest
   coal-burning power stations

H areas where there are several
   hydro-electric power stations

■ nuclear power stations

0   100   200
Km

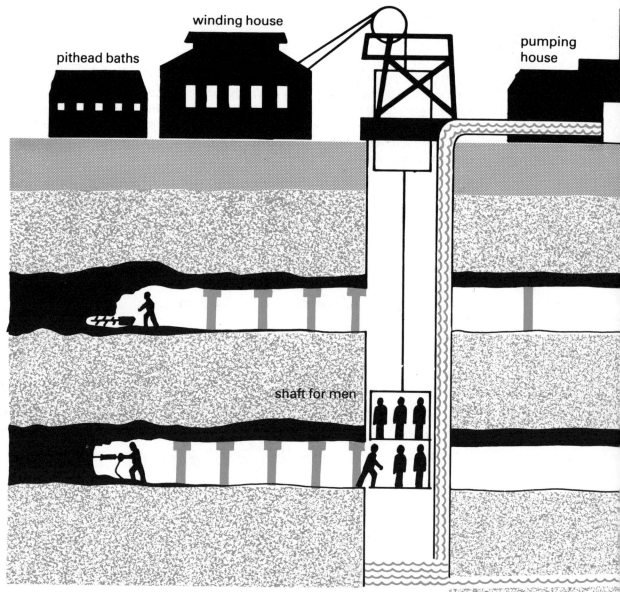

pithead baths

winding house

pumping house

shaft for men

Coalfields have been important to Britain for many hundreds of years. Even in the Middle Ages people complained about the smoke from the coal fires in private houses.

About three hundred years ago steam engines were first made to pump water and later used to power machines in factories. In 1709 Abraham Darby first smelted iron ore with coke. In the next two hundred years coal became easily the most important fuel in use in British factories. In the nineteenth century it powered steam engines which made the rail-

ways and the iron steamships possible. Coal gas, produced by baking coal in ovens, was supplied to towns and used for street lighting long before the discovery of electricity.

In the twentieth century steam power has gradually given way to a more convenient fuel – oil – in ships, on railways and in factories. As a result less coal has been needed. Moreover the use of natural gas instead of coal gas and the growth in the number of homes with central heating instead of coal fires have also meant that less coal is

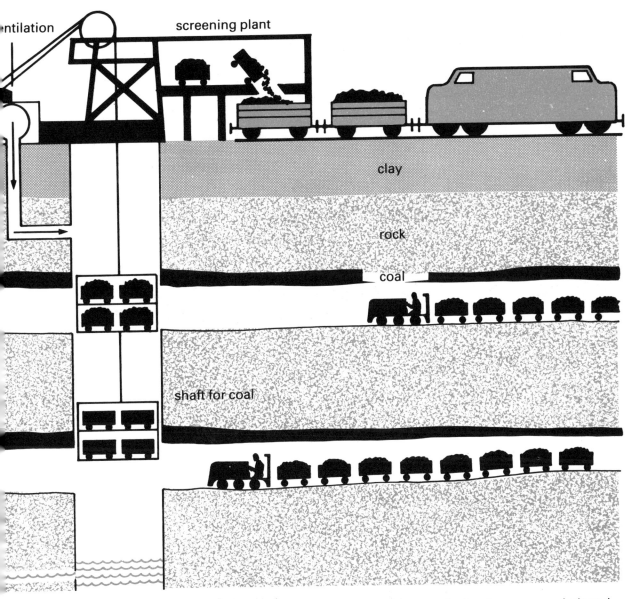

ventilation   screening plant

clay

rock

coal

shaft for coal

needed today. As a result the amount of coal produced in Britain has dropped by nearly half in the last twenty years or so.

The coal industry is still very important. Most of our electricity is generated by coal-burning power stations. There are still large amounts of coal left in Britain which can be mined. When all the world's oil and gas have been used up there will still be some coal left.

Modern collieries are very efficient and new mines are being opened to dig up newly-discovered seams of coal. The coal is dug out by machines and taken by conveyor belt and by underground railway to the pit shaft where it is pulled up in a lift to the pit head. In some modern mines there is a long sloping tunnel from the surface to the coal seams and this speeds up the way in which the coal is brought out of the mine. At the surface the coal goes on another conveyor to be washed and sorted into different sizes of coal.

Draw a series of pictures to show how coal is mined in a modern colliery today.

North sea oil and gas

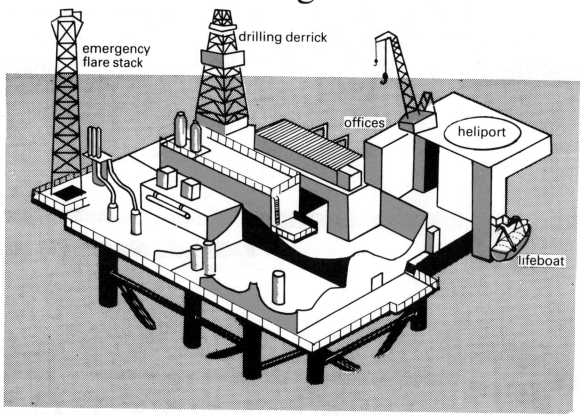

emergency flare stack

drilling derrick

offices

heliport

lifeboat

A hundred years ago much of Britain's wealth came from coal and iron. In the last fifty years coal has been replaced by oil as a source of power for many industries and machines. Until the 1970s oil had to be brought from the Middle East and from countries such as Venezuela and Nigeria. This meant that British goods had to be sold abroad to pay for it.

In the 1960s oil was discovered lying deep below the rocks under the North Sea. The oil companies discovered that there was enough oil there to provide Britain with all the oil she needed in the 1980s. Millions of pounds have been spent searching for this oil. Drilling platforms were erected, pipelines laid and special oil ports built to receive the oil when it came on shore. Thousands of people, particularly those living on the east coast of Scotland, got jobs in this new industry.

One of the hardest jobs of all is that of the workers on an oil rig who drill for oil. They live and work on their platform. A restaurant provides their meals and there are cinema shows and television sets on board. They go back to their homes at regular intervals travelling by helicopter.

Another hard job is that of the people who lay the pipelines on the bed of the sea. Deep-sea divers are needed for this work.

When the oil comes ashore it is piped or taken by tanker to refineries to be converted into petrol, diesel oil, lubricating oil and the thousands of other products which use oil as a raw material.

The first gas used in Britain was made by heating coal. It was called coal gas. Nowadays the gas used in Britain is found, like oil, in a natural state deep under the rocks. It is called natural gas. Not long ago all the natural gas used in Britain (like the oil) had to be brought into the country by ship from abroad. Today the gas comes from deposits under the North Sea and most of this comes ashore by pipeline.

In the map you can see where the main oil-fields are in the North Sea. The map also shows the areas which supply the natural gas used in Britain. Copy this map.

Copy the picture of an oil rig on the opposite page.

Write a few sentences to describe what it must be like living and working on such an oil rig in the middle of the winter.

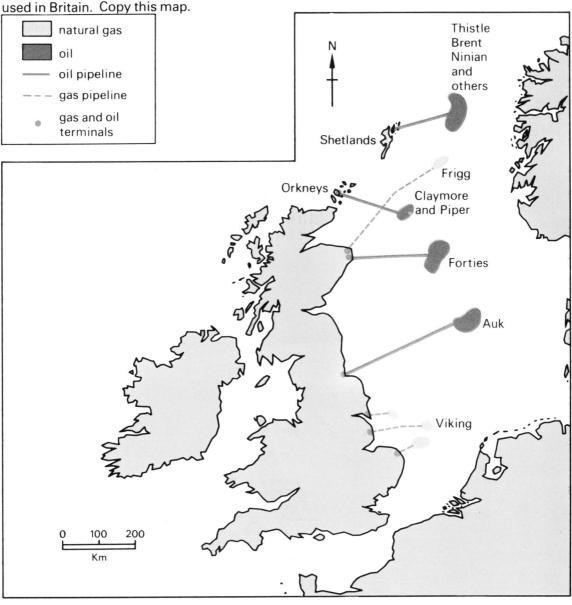

natural gas

oil

oil pipeline

gas pipeline

gas and oil terminals

N

Thistle
Brent
Ninian
and
others

Shetlands

Frigg

Orkneys

Claymore
and Piper

Forties

Auk

Viking

0   100   200
Km

Raw materials

Some of the raw materials used in industry occur naturally in the ground. They are called minerals because they are usually dug out from mines). Some minerals can be used as they are such as slate, rock salt or coal. Others have to be processed in order to get (extract) the mineral from the rock. The rock in which metals are found is called ore. Most ores have to be heated to a high temperature so that the metal melts and can then be collected separately from the rest of the earth.

Another source of raw materials is the produce from the land. Butter from milk, cloth from wool, beer from hops and barley, cider from apples and sugar from sugar beet are just a few of the foods and raw materials produced in Britain. Another raw material is timber for paper and furniture.

On the map you can see where some of Britain's raw materials come from. Some, such as coal and oil, are power sources as well. These raw materials come from Britain but many of those used in British factories have to be imported from abroad.

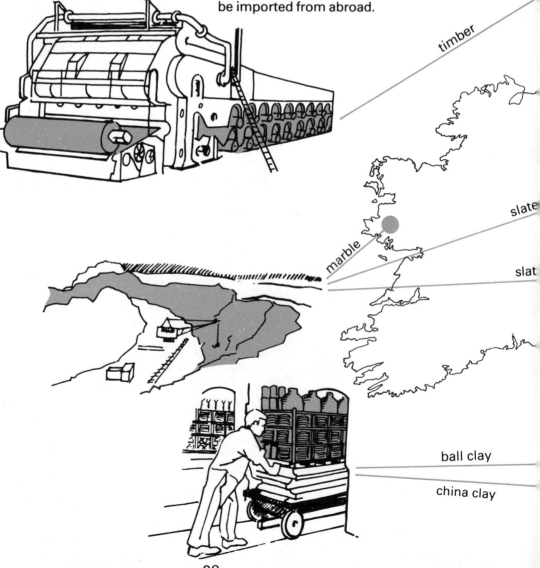

timber

slate

slat

marble

ball clay

china clay

N

oil

coal

anhydrite

salt

limestone

sugar beet

clay

chalk

0   100   200
Km

91

Iron and steel

The diagram below shows some of the processes involved in an iron and steel works. Look at this diagram carefully.

Make another copy of the diagram at the bottom of page 79.

Fill in the empty spaces with the names of the raw materials, sources of power, etc., which are used in an iron and steel works.

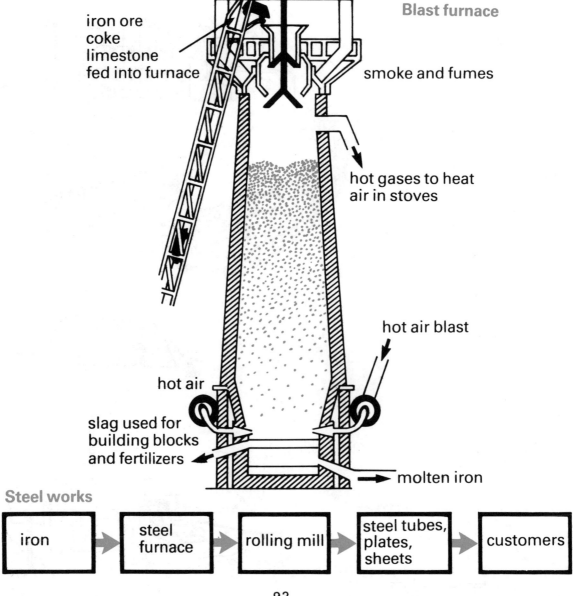

Blast furnace

iron ore
coke
limestone
fed into furnace

smoke and fumes

hot gases to heat
air in stoves

hot air blast

hot air

slag used for
building blocks
and fertilizers

molten iron

Steel works

| iron | → | steel furnace | → | rolling mill | → | steel tubes, plates, sheets | → | customers |

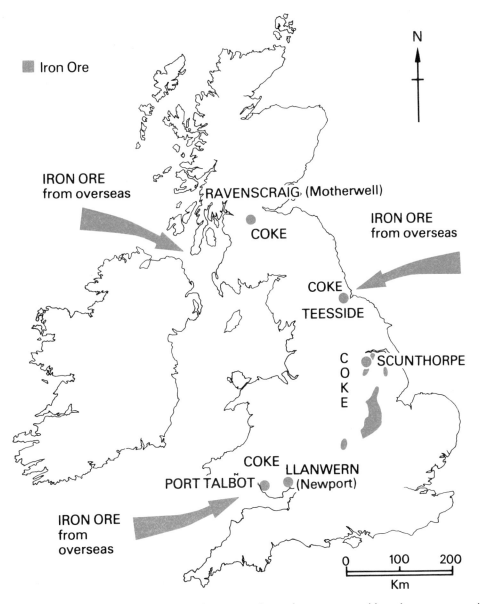

Iron Ore

IRON ORE from overseas

RAVENSCRAIG (Motherwell)
COKE

IRON ORE from overseas

COKE
TEESSIDE

C O K E
SCUNTHORPE

COKE
PORT TALBOT
LLANWERN (Newport)

IRON ORE from overseas

N

0   100   200
Km

In this map you can see where the main centres of the iron and steel industry are situated.

The steel industry is still the foundation for many industries such as those using steel plates, wire, tubing and girders as raw materials for their own products.

The steel industry in Britain is changing. In some parts of the country steel works have closed down whilst new up-to-date plants have been opened in other areas such as the Redcar Works on Teesside in Cleveland.

Copy this map. Look at the map of the coalfields on page 85.

Which iron-and-steel making centres are on or near coalfields?

Where are the other iron-and-steel making centres situated?

93

Metal industries

One of the main disadvantages of ordinary iron and steel is that they rust and only last a certain period of time. Some metals do not sharpen to a fine edge like steel but have other advantages (called properties) which may be more useful for certain products. For example some do not decay like rusting iron. Some can be easily shaped. Aluminium is light for its size whilst lead is heavy. Some metals can resist very high temperatures whilst mercury only becomes solid when very cold. As a result metals can be used to make many goods.

Until very recently metals had no competitors but the invention of many types of plastic has become a serious threat to the metal industries. Drainpipes are no longer made of metal and some car bodies are made from fibreglass (a product of the plastics industry).

The metal industries and those which use metals in their factories employ more workers in Britain than any other industry. These metal industries include factories making cars, engines, machines, refrigerators, washing machines, aircraft and ships. In fact metal industries are to be found in almost every town.

The maps show the main centres of two important metal industries—ship-building and the manufacture of motor vehicles.

The pictures opposite show what happens in a car factory. In a typical car you can find many metal products, and other raw materials. These include textiles (cloth for the seats), plastics, glass and sometimes wood.

The car industry is an assembly industry. Workers put together different parts (called components) which have been made elsewhere, either in other factories or in a separate part of the works.

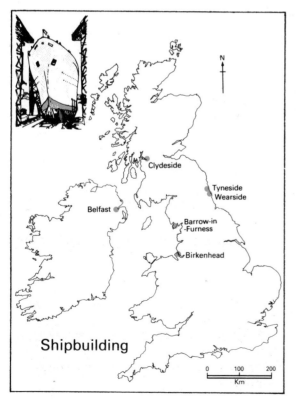

Shipbuilding

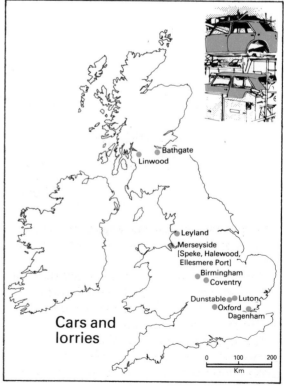

Cars and lorries

1. sheets of steel compressed to form car body in press shop

2. main parts of the car body welded together

3. body shell sprayed with paint

4. engine and gear box put together on assembly line

5. car body lowered onto engine

6. seats, carpets, instruments and other fittings complete the car

Chemical industries

The chemical industries provide many of the luxuries and essentials of modern living. Glass, aspirins, soap, explosives, medicines, plastics, nylon, table salt, carpets, oxygen, clothes, petrol, oil, paints, records and many other products are made in chemical works or from raw materials produced by the chemical industry.

The chemical industries take raw materials such as salt, limestone, water, coal, oil, gas, air, wood, sand and change them into other materials by chemical processes. These may involve using heat or cold, electricity, the effects of acid, and so on. These processes take place in huge tanks and pipes. Often the processes are controlled automatically. If you visited a chemical works you would see many white-coated scientists and skilled workers. Few jobs are done by hand. As a result the chemical industries usually employ relatively few people compared with some other industries. This is why the diagram on page 101 makes it look as if these are among the less important industries. In fact the value of the products of the chemical industries are very high. Many of the largest industrial companies in Britain make chemicals or chemical products or refine oil. They include firms like Shell, Unilever, British Petroleum (BP), I.C.I., Courtaulds, Boots, Beecham and British Oxygen.

This map shows where some of the most important chemical works are situated in Britain.

One of the biggest centres of the chemical industry in Britain is on Teesside in Cleveland where I.C.I. (Imperial Chemical Industries) have two giant works at Billingham and at Wilton. These plants cover a large area of land and millions of pounds have been spent on the buildings and equipment there. Teesside also has an oil refinery.

The main advantage of Teesside for a chemical industry was that the Billingham works was built over the site of supplies of anhydrite, a chemical which could be pro-

cessed to make sulphur (for ammonia and fertilisers). It was also close to coal mined on the Durham coalfield nearby. After the Second World War a new chemical works was built at Wilton because oil could be brought up the Tees estuary and piped to the works. These two works were able to make use of a number of essential raw materials. Being close together meant that a pipeline could connect the two works enabling raw materials to be taken from one site to the other almost as if they were both built on the same plot of land.

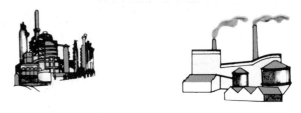

oil refineries

main centres of chemical works

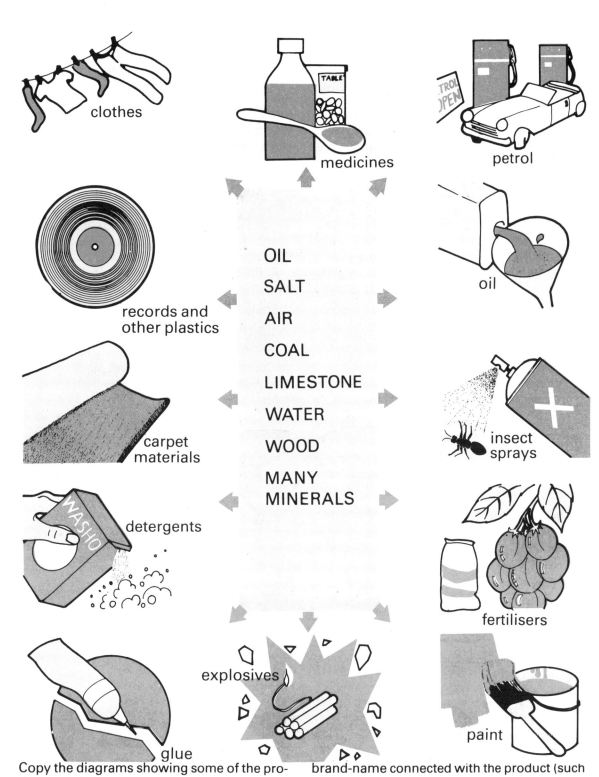

clothes

medicines

petrol

OIL
SALT
AIR
COAL
LIMESTONE
WATER
WOOD
MANY
MINERALS

records and
other plastics

oil

carpet
materials

insect
sprays

detergents

fertilisers

glue

explosives

paint

Copy the diagrams showing some of the products made by chemical industries. Write against each product the name of a firm or a brand-name connected with the product (such as **Esso** petrol or **Castrol XL** oil).

Textiles

The textiles and clothing industry is probably older than the metal industry – especially in Britain. Primitive people needed warm clothing. At first this came from the furs and skins of wild animals. When they learned how to herd sheep primitive people were able to spin and weave wool for clothing.

For three thousand years woollen cloth was Britain's most important industry. When explorers brought back cotton from hotter lands and showed how its white fibre (like cotton-wool) could be spun into cotton a new textile industry was born. Textiles is the name given to materials which can be woven into cloth. The materials are called fibres. They consist of strands of material which can be twisted together to make them stronger and then spun out to make thread.

The main cotton industry grew up in Lancashire near to the port of Liverpool through which the cotton was imported. The coal on the Lancashire coalfield was used at first to heat the water which was used to wash the cloth and dye it. Later it was used to power steam engines which turned the machines. The Lancashire cotton industry grew much faster than other industries in Britain in the eighteenth and nineteenth centuries and many large towns grew up there. You can see these towns, such as Oldham, Bolton, Burnley and Blackburn on the map opposite.

At the same time the woollen and worsted industry (a different type of cloth made from wool) grew rapidly in Yorkshire in towns like Bradford, Halifax and Huddersfield. Other woollen industries in Britain such as those in Norfolk and in the West Country could not produce cloth as cheaply. This was partly because they were a long distance away from the coalfields.

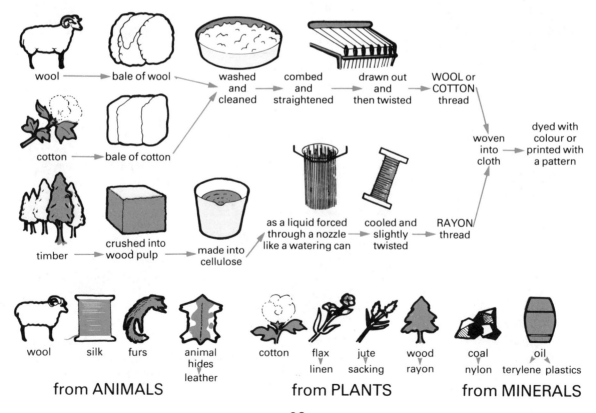

wool → bale of wool → washed and cleaned → combed and straightened → drawn out and then twisted → WOOL or COTTON thread

cotton → bale of cotton

timber → crushed into wood pulp → made into cellulose → as a liquid forced through a nozzle like a watering can → cooled and slightly twisted → RAYON thread

woven into cloth → dyed with colour or printed with a pattern

wool   silk   furs   animal hides leather
from ANIMALS

cotton   flax linen   jute sacking   wood rayon
from PLANTS

coal nylon   oil terylene plastics
from MINERALS

98

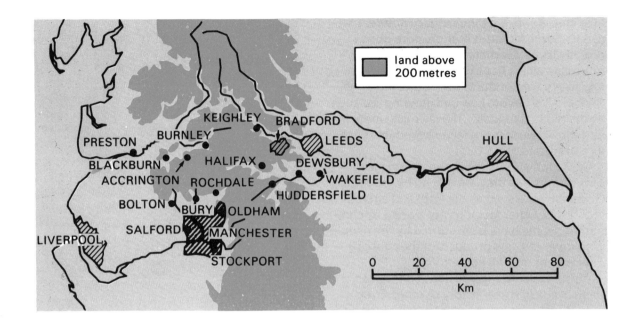

land above 200 metres

KEIGHLEY BRADFORD
PRESTON BURNLEY LEEDS HULL
BLACKBURN HALIFAX DEWSBURY
ACCRINGTON ROCHDALE WAKEFIELD
BOLTON HUDDERSFIELD
BURY OLDHAM
SALFORD MANCHESTER
LIVERPOOL STOCKPORT

0   20   40   60   80
Km

Today the textile industries of both Lancashire and Yorkshire are no longer as important as they once were. Towns like Blackburn and Huddersfield have many other industries. Many mills were closed down years ago. One reason for this was that in the past much of the cloth that was produced was sold abroad. Countries which used to buy British cloth either began to make it themselves or were able to buy it at a much cheaper price from countries like Japan. Another reason was that new man-made fibres were discovered. These are fibres made by machines.

Oil and coal were used to produce new materials such as terylene (from oil) and nylon (from coal).

Scientists discovered they could make a new fibre called rayon from the cellulose in timber or from poor quality cotton.

Many of the mills of Lancashire and Yorkshire used these man-made fibres in a mixture (or blend) with cotton or wool to make new cloths (or fabrics as they are often called). Nowadays there is no longer any need to make textiles in Lancashire and Yorkshire. Modern textile mills use electricity, oil and gas as sources of power. The raw materials they use can be taken anywhere in Britain. Many textile factories making man-made fibres have been built well outside this area for this reason. But many textile works still remain. This is because once an industry has become fixed in one area it is likely to remain there long after the reasons for setting it up in the first place have disappeared. Only when there are big disadvantages in continuing to manufacture those goods in that area is the industry likely to move. Other industries which are like this include the cutlery industry of Sheffield and the pottery industry of Stoke-on-Trent.

Many industries

It is impossible to study every single industry in Britain. There are thousands of different factories. Some factories manufacture goods directly from raw materials. Others use raw materials which have been partly processed and many use products from other factories. Some industries are new and growing fast such as the plastics industry, the chemical industry and those which manufacture products such as computers.

Some industries have been nationalised. This means that they are owned by the British Government – such as the steel and aircraft industries. Other factories are owned by companies. Some have been started by the people who invented new products or thought of a new way of making something.

Almost everything you use at home has been made in some factory or other. Even something simple such as a table set for a meal (shown in the picture below) draws from a number of different industries. The picture shows where some of these products are made in Britain although bear in mind that similar products are made in other parts of Britain and the world.

On the opposite page you can see that the matchstick figures show roughly how many people work in each industry in Britain. Each matchstick figure represents 250,000 workers.

Which industry employs most workers? Add up all the industries which use metals as their main raw materials. How many matchstick figures does it total? How many people does this represent if each figure represents 250,000 workers? Copy this table.

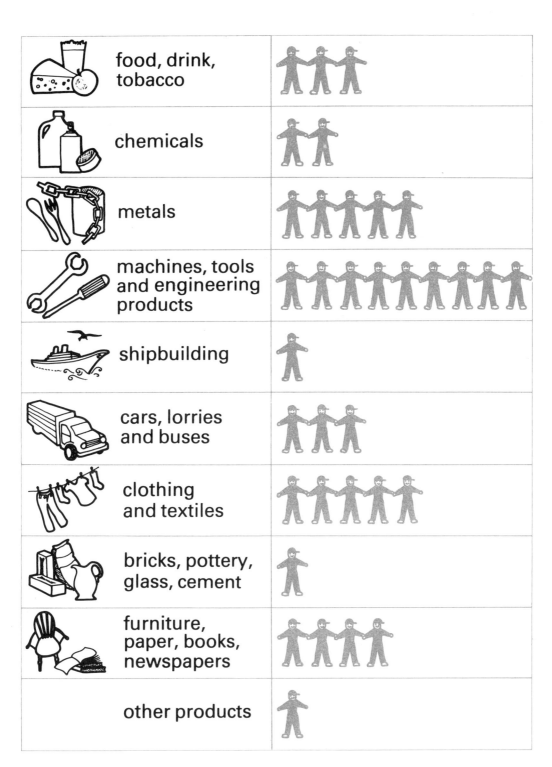	food, drink, tobacco	
	chemicals	
	metals	
	machines, tools and engineering products	
	shipbuilding	
	cars, lorries and buses	
	clothing and textiles	
	bricks, pottery, glass, cement	
	furniture, paper, books, newspapers	
	other products	

Exercises

1. Why is coal still important today?

2. Where are most of the big power stations situated in Britain?

3. How do nuclear power stations work?

4. Where are most of the nuclear power stations situated in Britain?

5. What natural force is used by hydro-electric power stations?

6. Where are most of the hydro-electric power stations situated in Britain?

7. Name three oilfields in the North Sea.

8. Copy the map below.
   Name on your map the type of power source shown by the letters A, B, C, D, E.

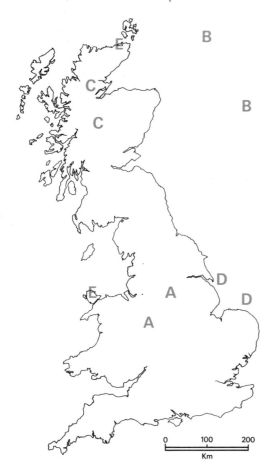

9. What are the main raw materials of (a) the iron and steel industry (b) the chemical industries?

10. What substance is the basis of the plastics industry?

11. What is an assembly industry? Give the names of three examples of assembly industries.

12. Copy the diagram at the top of the opposite page.
    Write in the spaces on your diagram the names of the industries which provided these parts of the car.

13. Write out an alphabet of British industries and products starting with AEROPLANES, BRICKS and CARS and finishing with YACHTS and ZIP FASTENERS.

14. Look at the statements below. Which statements are TRUE and which are FALSE? write the statements out so that they all read correctly.
    (a) Raw materials are the things from which other goods can be made.
    (b) The main sources of power in British factories are coal and steam power.
    (c) A factory needs good roads and usually good canal and sea communications as well.

15. Copy the diagram at the foot of page 103 and fill in the blanks to show what happens when cloth made from wool is manufactured.

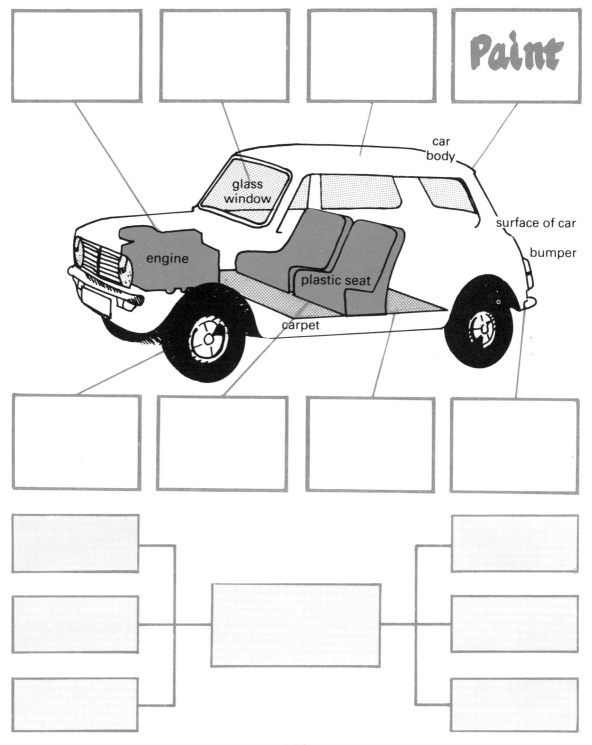

Paint

car body

glass window

surface of car

bumper

engine

plastic seat

carpet

TRANSPORT

Roads

The first motorway in Britain was opened in 1958. Since then many other motorways have been built. Most of the large cities are close to a motorway linking them to other cities and to London. There are over 2000km of motorways in Britain and nearly 350 000km of other roads.

On the map opposite you can see where these motorways are situated in Britain. The advantages brought by the motorways are many. They include (a) speeding up the delivery of goods by heavy lorries (b) cutting down the number of traffic jams on older roads (c) safer motoring at speed. Motorways are safer for high speed traffic because the vehicles on one carriageway all go in the same direction. Traffic enters or leaves a motorway on the left so ensuring that no traffic ever turns right across the direction in which other vehicles are travelling. The carriageways are usually much wider than on ordinary roads, there are no traffic lights or pedestrian crossings or roundabouts forcing traffic to halt and the gradients and bends on the motorways are usually so gentle high speed traffic does not have to slow down. Because of this the motorways take up much more land than do ordinary roads. Since they are almost always completely new roads this means that valuable countryside is lost whenever a motorway is built. Since the gradients and bends have to be gentle the motorway engineers have to plan the direction of the road carefully and this means choosing routes which avoid the need to move great quantities of earth.

Copy the map opposite and mark on it the position of your town or village (or that of a town or village where a relative lives).

Which is the nearest motorway to the town or village you have marked on the map?

Which motorway or motorways would you drive on from that town or village if you were driving (a) to Exeter (b) to London (c) to Manchester?

Which areas of Britain are without motorways? Why is this?

Which areas of Britain are best served by motorways? Why is this?

Perth
M85
M9 M90
M8 · Edinburgh
M8 · Glasgow

Newcastle
upon Tyne
Carlisle
A1(M)
Scarborough
M6
York
Leeds M62
M66
M62 Hull
Liverpool M18
M53 M56
Manchester
M1
M6
M6
Birmingham
M5
Norwich
M50
M1
Cambridge
Gloucester M11
Oxford London
M4 M40
Cardiff M2
Bristol Reading
M25 M20 Dover
M3 M23
M5
M27 M27
Exeter Southampton Brighton
Portsmouth
Truro ·
Plymouth

0   100   200
Km

Railways

The map on the opposite page shows the railway services in Great Britain in 1978–79. The lines show the main Inter-City services. These are the services between London and the important towns.

As you can see large areas of Wales and Scotland and country areas in Devonshire and East Anglia have very few railways. This is because railway services only make money when there are lots of passengers. About twenty years ago a lot of stations were closed. Today the railways have been streamlined. Special trains called freightliners carry goods in special containers to factories and to the ports. Many railway lines have been electrified. The latest express train services from London to Bristol and to Scotland are very fast indeed.

Copy the map opposite and mark on it the position of your town or village (or that of a town or village where a relative lives).

Is the town or village you have marked close to an Inter-City train service?

Compare the map you have drawn of the railways with that you drew of the motorways of Britain (see page 105).

What similarities and what differences are there?

Are the areas *without* Inter-City services the same as those without motorways?

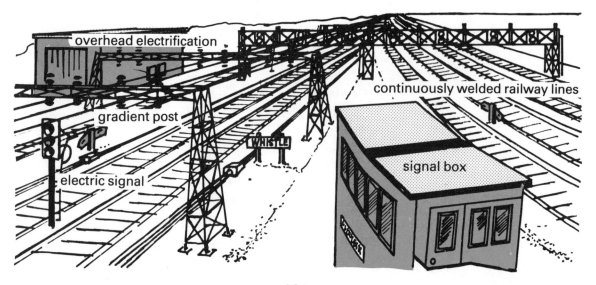

Inter-City lines

Inverness
Aberdeen
Dundee
Perth
Glasgow
Edinburgh
Berwick
Kilmarnock
Newcastle
Carlisle
Darlington
York
Leeds
Hull
Preston
Manchester
Doncaster
Grimsby
Liverpool
Sheffield
Holyhead
Crewe
Derby
King's Lynn
Leicester
Norwich
Shrewsbury
Birmingham
Cambridge
Colchester
Fishguard
Gloucester
Harwich
Swansea
Oxford
London
Margate
Cardiff
Swindon
Reading
Bristol
Dover
Taunton
Southampton
Portsmouth
Hastings
Exeter
Brighton
Plymouth
Weymouth
Penzance

Ports

Many of the most important British towns are ports. They include London, Liverpool, Manchester, Glasgow, Cardiff, Belfast and Dublin. Some towns grew in importance as ports for the navy such as Plymouth and Portsmouth. Others grew as ports from which passengers could sail to America (Southampton) or to Europe (Dover and Harwich) or between Great Britain and Ireland (Stranraer, Larne, Heysham, Holyhead, Dun Laoghaire, Rosslare and Fishguard).

These ports have been affected by recent changes. Nowadays it is much easier for trade to be carried out in container ships. Containers are the large oblong chests you can see on lorries on fast motor roads. They are loaded at the factory and need not then be unpacked until they reach the end of their journeys. Because they are the same shape they can be carried by lorry, railway truck or by boat. Special container ports have grown rapidly as a result of this change. This has been at the expense of the old ports which still use cranes and load and unload in the old way.

The map opposite shows the position of the most important ports in Britain.

Copy this map and mark on it the position of your town or village (or that of a town or village where a relative lives).

Which is the nearest port to the town or village you have marked on the map?

Look at the maps you drew showing motorways (see page 105) and showing railways (see page 107).

Which ports are particularly well-served by railways and motorways?

Which is the easiest route from the town or village you have marked by motorway or by railway to (a) a port on the west coast (e.g. Bristol, Liverpool, Glasgow) (b) a port on the east coast (e.g. London, Hull)?

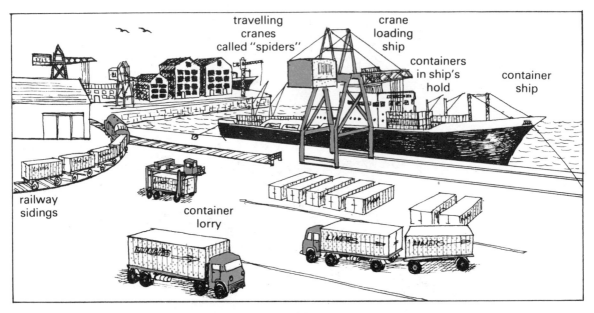

travelling cranes called "spiders"

crane loading ship

containers in ship's hold

container ship

railway sidings

container lorry

N

Glasgow   Leith

■ naval
▲ ferry terminal
● ports

Larne   Stranraer

Belfast

Teesside

Douglas

Hull

Immingham   Manchester
Liverpool

Dublin
Dun Laoghaire   Holyhead

Felixstowe
Harwich

Rosslare

Cork   Fishguard
Bantry Bay   Milford Haven   Tilbury
Swansea   London   Chatham
Bristol   Medway
Dover
Folkestone
Southampton   Newhaven
Portsmouth
Plymouth   Weymouth

0   100   200
Km

Airways

Air transport has grown rapidly in the last thirty years. Today it is so fast and so safe that it is often the only way you can travel to distant places. The busiest airport in Britain (and in Europe) is London's Heathrow airport.

Travel by air between different places within Britain is not so important as it is in a larger country. This is because airports are almost always some distance away from city centres. It is often cheaper, easier and nearly as quick to travel by rail from city centre to city centre where the direct rail journeys are short. The most important air services are between the mainland of Great Britain and Ireland and other islands such as the Channel Islands, Isle of Man, Hebrides, Orkneys and Shetlands.

The map opposite shows the main airports in Britain.

Copy this map and mark on it the position of your town or village (or that of a town or village where a relative lives).

Which is the nearest airport to the town or village you have marked on the map?

Canals

Between 1760 and 1840 many hundreds of kilometres of canals were dug in Britain to enable heavy raw materials like coal and iron ore to be carried cheaply from one area to another. The coming of the railways and later of the motor vehicle meant that canal traffic was unable to compete. Canal barges were so much slower that the savings in transport costs were no longer so important.

Recently some canals have shown signs of regaining some of their old prosperity. In Europe canal barges carry a lot of goods and raw materials. Special boats have been built to take these barges straight from Europe across the sea to British canal ports. In this way goods carried in barges do not have to be unloaded until they reach their final destination.

N

Aberdeen

Glasgow
Edinburgh

Prestwick

Newcastle

Belfast

Teesside

Isle of Man

Leeds

Liverpool

Dublin

Manchester

East Midlands

Shannon

Birmingham

Stansted

Luton

Southend

Cork

Swansea

Cardiff

Bristol

Heathrow

Gatwick

Airports

Southampton

Bournemouth

Plymouth

0   100   200
Km

Tourism

The tourist industry is one of Britain's most important industries. It is dependent on good means of transport.

Each year several million foreign visitors go to London first – if only because they fly to Heathrow Airport. After London they head for historic towns and cities like Edinburgh, Stratford-upon-Avon, Bath, Oxford, Cambridge, Dublin and York.

British holidaymakers still travel to the seaside resorts round the coast. The seaside was not thought of as a place for holidays until about 250 years ago when the new turnpike roads were built and when stage coach and mail coach services made it easier to travel long distances. They were expensive journeys however and only the well-to-do could afford a holiday at the seaside. When railway lines were built to the coast from the industrial towns it was possible for factory workers to take cheap excursions to the seaside. As a result many seaside resorts grew into large towns. Although many British people go abroad seaside resorts like Brighton, Blackpool, Southend, Bournemouth, Torquay and Scarborough continue to flourish.

The map on the opposite page shows some of the most important seaside resorts in the British Isles.

Although a good sandy beach and hot sunny summers are big advantages they are not the only reasons why resorts become popular. Many big resorts have poor beaches.

The most important reason is the distance from the resort to the places where most people live. This was much more important in the past than it is today. Then the resorts which were closest to the big cities and towns grew much more quickly than those which were a long distance away. Londoners could travel to Brighton, Margate and Southend easily by train. It took longer to get to Cromer on the Norfolk coast. Lancashire workers flocked to Blackpool or Southport whilst Yorkshire workers went to Scarborough or Bridlington.

Today many people go by car on holiday and resorts a long distance away from the big towns have flourished such as Newquay in Cornwall. They have gained particularly from the opening up of new motorways.

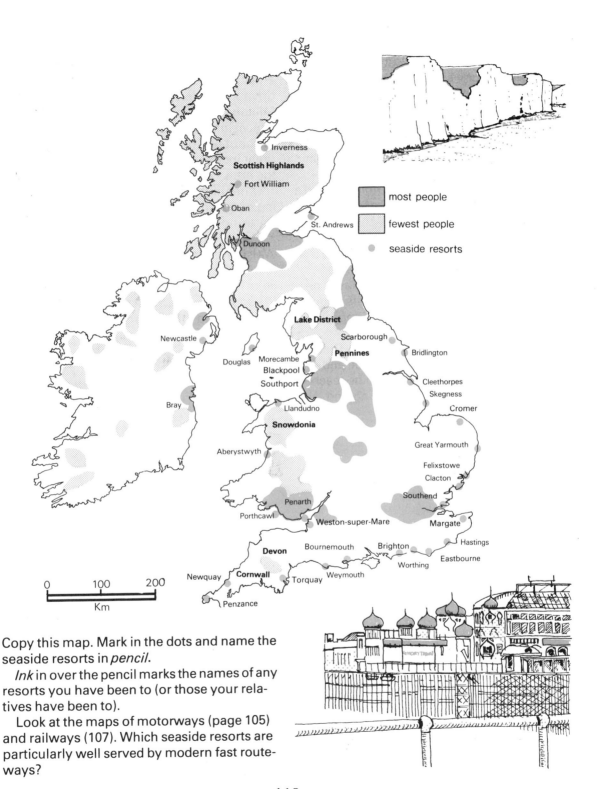

most people	(shaded)
fewest people	(dotted)
seaside resorts	(dot)

Inverness

Scottish Highlands

Fort William

Oban

St. Andrews

Dunoon

Lake District

Scarborough

Newcastle

Bridlington

Douglas

Morecambe

Pennines

Blackpool

Southport

Cleethorpes

Skegness

Llandudno

Cromer

Snowdonia

Bray

Great Yarmouth

Aberystwyth

Felixstowe

Clacton

Southend

Penarth

Porthcawl

Margate

Weston-super-Mare

Hastings

Devon

Bournemouth

Brighton

Worthing

Eastbourne

Newquay

Cornwall

Torquay

Weymouth

Penzance

0   100   200
Km

Copy this map. Mark in the dots and name the seaside resorts in *pencil*.

Ink in over the pencil marks the names of any resorts you have been to (or those your relatives have been to).

Look at the maps of motorways (page 105) and railways (107). Which seaside resorts are particularly well served by modern fast routeways?

The mountains and hills of Britain are another big attraction for visitors. Motorists, climbers, canoeists and campers are some of the tourists who crowd into the mountain holiday areas such as the Lake District in England, Snowdonia in Wales, the Kerry Mountains in the Irish Republic and the Scottish Highlands. In Scotland the snow on the Grampian mountains is often suitable for skiing holidays and a ski lift has been built at Aviemore for winter sports visitors.

Many highland areas like Snowdonia, the Peak District of the Pennines and the Lake District have been made into National Parks. Within these parks restrictions are placed on new buildings, the placing of advertisements and many other things which could spoil these beautiful areas.

The main tourist centres in the Lake District are at Keswick, Grasmere, Ambleside and Windermere. The Lake District can be reached quickly by car by most people in England. A dual carriageway joins the southern part of the area to the M6 motorway. Londoners can now drive to Windermere in about four hours. Millions of people living in the Midlands, Lancashire and Yorkshire can reach the Lakes in about two hours or so. This has meant a great increase in the number of day visitors to the area.

Other highland areas affected by the opening of new motorways have been Exmoor and Dartmoor in the West Country.

Snowdonia, the main holiday area in the Welsh mountains, is not so easily reached by fast motor roads. In Ireland Killarney is the chief holiday centre for the Kerry Mountains in the south-west. In Scotland there are several important holiday centres. Thousands of visitors go each year to places like Fort William, Oban, Inverness, Pitlochry and Aviemore. The highland areas of Scotland cover a much bigger area than those in other parts of Britain.

Exercises

1. Look at the statements below. Which statements are TRUE and which are FALSE? Write the statements out so that they all read correctly.
   (a) There are over 350 000km of motorways in Britain.
   (b) Country areas in Wales, Scotland, Devonshire and East Anglia have very few railways.
   (c) Plymouth and Portsmouth are naval ports.
   (d) The busiest airport in Britain is Ringway Airport in Manchester.
   (e) Canals in Britain are no longer used for carrying goods.
   (f) Snowdonia and the Lake District are National Parks.

2. Which areas of Britain are best served by motorways, railways, ports and airports? Why?

3. Name two advantages of (a) motorways (b) containers.

4. Copy the map below and print in correctly the names of the three airports marked by aeroplane symbols.
   Draw in and label correctly the M1 and M6 motorways.
   Mark and name Glasgow, Manchester, Leeds, Sheffield, Birmingham, Bristol and London
   Print the letter A over three areas which are badly served by motorways and Inter-City railway services.

N

0   100   200
Km

115

TOWNS

Sites of towns

The place or plot of land where a town has grown up is called its site.

Sometimes the site of a town is on a steep slope (as at Halifax). Usually very steep slopes are avoided. Sometimes the site of the town or village is on a hill top (as at Stow-on-the-Wold in the Cotswolds). In the past people often took advantage of hill tops as a place to build a village because it could be easily defended there. Sometimes the bend of a river made another site which could be easily defended. The town grew up within the bend so that there was water on three sides. Often a castle was built on the fourth side. Towns like this include Durham and Shrewsbury. Sometimes you can see remains of the old town walls.

Some of the most common types of site for a town and some of the places which were avoided are shown in the pictures opposite.

What type of town site is shown in this photograph?

How towns have grown

Most of the towns and cities in Britain were once villages. Only a few were intended as towns right from the start. There were usually good reasons why some villages grew into towns while the rest stayed as they were. The towns had advantages which helped them to become busy places.

Being on a river helped many towns to grow. The river could be used for the water supply. Sometimes it was used to turn a waterwheel in a mill. Boats used the river to bring goods to and from the town. The roads often followed the river valley because it was low down.

Many rivers could only be crossed in one or two places. Sometimes there were fords if the river was shallow enough to be crossed on horseback. Sometimes there were bridges. The importance of being able to cross a river is seen in the number of towns which have ford or bridge in their names like Oxford and Cambridge.

Some villages grew into towns because they were good places to hold a market. In the old days there were not many shops and people bought many of the things they wanted at the market. Many of these old towns had workshops where craftsmen made cloth, knives and other goods. There were no big factories.

About two or three hundred years ago coal was first used to make steam to provide power for machines. Large mills and factories had to be built in order to use these machines. Many factories were built and new coal mines were dug. The towns situated near the coalfields of Lancashire and Yorkshire grew rapidly as people came to work in the mines and factories.

Some towns grew up because they had special industries such as the pottery industry at Stoke-on-Trent and the woollen industry at Bradford in Yorkshire.

Most towns had a special reason like this for growing into important, busy centres. You will read about some of these special types of town on pages 120–121.

1. village by a river

4. village gets the right to hold a market – is now a small town

7. town factories specialise in making cloth

As they grew the towns became important in other ways. Shopkeepers saw that a growing town was a good place in which to build a new shop. Town-centre shops were then visited by people from outside the town. Buses and trains made it possible for country people to travel a long way in order to do business or to shop. So Stoke-on-Trent and Bradford have also grown because they are shopping centres as well as being industrial towns. The industries and the shops made it likely that banks and other offices would be set up in the towns as well. The largest town in the area was also the best place for a warehouse or for the headquarters of any business which needed a centre from which to serve the people living nearby.

Today all large towns have a number of jobs to do. These jobs are often called the functions of the town. These functions include administrative (governing the area), residential (providing homes for the townspeople), shopping, business (banks and offices), transport (bus and railway centres), entertainment (cinemas, cafes and clubs) and industrial.

What town functions are performed in these buildings?

TOWN HALL	POWER STATION	AIRPORT	MECCA BALLROOM
MIDLAND BANK	BLOCK OF FLATS	CATHEDRAL	WOOLWORTH'S STORE

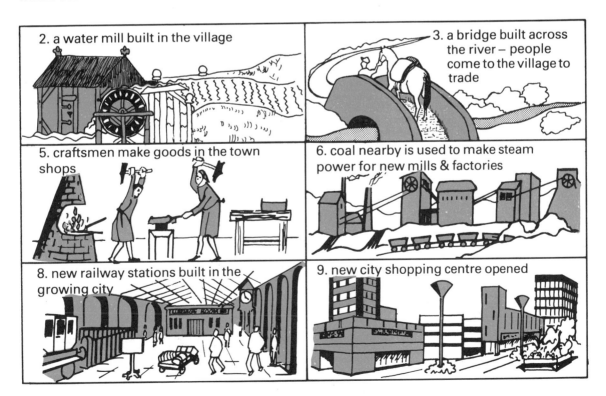

2. a water mill built in the village

3. a bridge built across the river – people come to the village to trade

5. craftsmen make goods in the town shops

6. coal nearby is used to make steam power for new mills & factories

8. new railway stations built in the growing city

9. new city shopping centre opened

Types of towns

The towns of Britain can be divided into different types according to the main jobs or functions they do. The most common types of town are the industrial towns and the market towns.

There are market towns in every area. People need somewhere to shop. The market towns were originally villages which had the right to hold markets and fairs. Markets like these were needed at regular intervals throughout the country in the days when there were no buses, cars and trains. People wanted to be within walking distance of the market.

Nowadays market town has come to mean any small town which is the chief shopping centre for the district whether or not it still has a market.

Almost all towns have industries. Even cities like Cambridge with its university or towns like Brighton, famous as a seaside resort, have important industries as well.

Some industries are, or were, so important to a town that the industry became associated with the town or its area as around Stoke-on-Trent which is often called, 'The Potteries' and Birmingham and district known as 'The Black Country'. There are shipbuilding towns like Barrow-in-Furness, Wallsend, and Birkenhead; woollen towns like Huddersfield and Halifax; cotton towns like Oldham and Blackburn; coal-mining towns like Barnsley and Bishop Auckland; steel towns like Sheffield, Scunthorpe and Consett. Today many of these industries are no longer the only important occupations of the townspeople. Most towns tend to have a range of industries today.

Some towns are tourist centres.

It is easy to recognise seaside resorts for this is a function which is unmistakable. Resorts like Brighton, Blackpool and Bournemouth are also business and shopping centres for their areas. They also have some industries and are the homes of commuters who work elsewhere.

Some towns like Crewe, Swindon and Darlington grew up as railway towns with large railway workshops and extensive railway sidings. Some modern towns are now growing faster as a result of their position close to the motorways.

University towns like Cambridge, Oxford and St Andrews in Scotland grew up originally because of the presence of the university there.

Cathedral cities and county towns like Lincoln, Norwich, Exeter, Worcester, Hereford, Gloucester, Chichester, Canterbury, Durham, Chester and Winchester often have many fine old buildings. They are old towns. Today their industries and shops are of greater importance than their functions as cathedral cities.

As you have already seen many towns are ports such as the naval ports (Plymouth), cross-Channel ports (Dover), transatlantic ports (Southampton), fishing ports (Grimsby) and the big general cargo ports like Hull and Liverpool.

What types of towns are shown in the drawings on these pages?
Copy these pictures. Label each picture with the type of town it represents. Give the names of *two* examples of towns like this in Britain.

Towns of Britain

Most people in Britain live in a town. Only a small number live on farms and in villages.

Some towns are by themselves such as Plymouth in Devonshire. Other towns are part of a group of towns. They join on to one another. When travelling through the area round Manchester for instance it is easy to go through places like Oldham, Stockport and Bolton without always realising where the town ends and the towns and suburbs closer to Manchester begin. These large built-up areas containing several towns or a large number of suburbs are called conurbations.

By far the largest conurbation in Britain is Greater London. It contains over 7 million people including many large important towns such as Croydon. The next largest conurbations are those of Greater Manchester and the West Midlands area around Birmingham. Greater Manchester includes Bolton, Bury, Oldham, Rochdale, Salford, Stockport, Tameside, Trafford and Wigan. The West Midlands includes Birmingham, Coventry, Dudley, Sandwell, Solihull, Walsall and Wolverhampton. Both conurbations have nearly 3 million people each.

Other great conurbations are those of West Yorkshire (Leeds and Bradford), Strathclyde (Glasgow), Merseyside (Liverpool), South Yorkshire (Sheffield) and Tyne and Wear (Newcastle-upon-Tyne). Four people out of every ten living in Britain live in one of these conurbations.

The map opposite shows the largest towns in Britain.
Copy this map.
Look at the map of the coalfields on page 85. Which of the towns on the map on this page are not situated on or close to a coalfield? Make a list of them.
Which of the towns on your list are not situated at the coast?

N

Aberdeen

Dundee

Edinburgh

Glasgow

Belfast

Newcastle-upon-Tyne
Sunderland
Carlisle
Middlesbrough

York
Blackpool   Bradford   Leeds   Hull
Preston   Huddersfield   Barnsley
           Bolton   Manchester   Doncaster
Liverpool   Sheffield
Dublin   Birkenhead   Stockport

Stoke   Nottingham
              Derby
                                      Norwich
                    Leicester
Wolverhampton
Birmingham   Coventry
                              Cambridge   Ipswich
Cork
                         Oxford   Southend
Swansea   Newport
         Cardiff   Reading   London
              Bristol

Southampton   Portsmouth   Brighton
Bournemouth

Plymouth

0   100   200
Km

123

Modern towns

Most towns are old and only a few have become towns in the present century. After the Second World War new towns were deliberately built to take some of the population of the big conurbations and make them less crowded. Some new towns started as villages such as Peterlee in County Durham. Others started as small towns like Stevenage in Hertfordshire and Harlow in Essex. They are almost always industrial centres with brand new housing estates, schools and shopping centres. The map on the opposite page shows the new towns built in Britain since 1945.

Older towns have been improved by building new suburbs with gardens and trees. Many areas of bad housing and old factories close to the centres of old towns have been pulled down and redeveloped. New buildings such as flats, shops and offices have been erected in their place. This is called urban renewal. On the outskirts of most large cities areas have been named as green belts. This is to prevent building up even further the spread of the towns. It means that no new buildings can be erected in a wide band all the way round a town thus ensuring that the townspeople are still close to the countryside. In many conurbations people live a long way from fields and farms simply because the towns were allowed to grow in the past without hindrance.

New industries have been attracted to special sites called trading estates usually built close to main roads. In some parts of the country the old industries have lost their importance and many people have become unemployed. To attract new industries some of these areas have been called Development Areas. This means that special terms are offered to persuade manufacturers to build new factories there.

A trading estate

New towns

New towns

● Expected to have less than 100,000 people

□ Expected to have between 100,000 & 200,000 people

■ Expected to have more than 200,000 people

Glenrothes
Cumbernauld
East Kilbride
Irvine
Livingston

Washington
Peterlee
Aycliffe

Central Lancashire
Skelmersdale
Warrington
Runcorn

Telford
Peterborough
Corby
Newtown
Redditch
Northampton
Milton Keynes
Stevenage
Welwyn Garden City
Harlow
Hemel Hempstead
Cwmbran
Hatfield
Basildon
Bracknell
Crawley

N

0   100   200
Km

Copy this map.

Mark on it the position of your town or village (or that of a town or village where a relative lives).

Which is the nearest new town to the town or village you have marked on the map?

Which large cities are close to these new towns?

Which new towns have taken some of the population of (a) London (b) Birmingham (c) Liverpool (d) Glasgow (e) Newcastle-upon-Tyne?

London

London is a huge city. Its importance comes partly from the fact that it was a good place to cross the Thames many hundreds of years ago. It was also a good place to sail a boat to since the estuary of the Thames was sheltered from storms. This meant that it had big advantages as a port since goods could be brought here from the country north of the Thames and also from the country south of the Thames. The two areas were joined by the bridge across the Thames.

In the Middle Ages it became the capital of England. This meant that the King and his Government and Parliament had their headquarters in London. People always regarded London as the most important city even in Roman times. Thousands of crafts made London an industrial town in medieval times and today it has many factories and works. London's history attracts tourists from all over the world. Foreign holidaymakers visit London first of all. Many arrive at Heathrow Airport, the busiest in Europe. London's mainline railway stations like Liverpool Street, King's Cross, Euston, Paddington, Victoria and Waterloo carry millions of passengers each year.

In the City of London every important business in Britain and almost every important bank in the world has an office. This is the centre of big business. London also has two cathedrals, a great abbey and three universities. It has many more theatres, museums and art galleries than any other town in Britain. It is also by far the most important shopping centre with many huge department stores.

Why is London like almost all the other types of towns put together?
Write out a list of the different functions you can see in these pictures of London.

Exercises

1. What is the land on which a town or village is situated called?

2. Why were some villages and towns built on the tops of hills?

3. Why were many towns situated on rivers? Give five reasons.

4. What is a market town?

5. What are the main functions of a town?

6. Look at the picture below.
   Trace the outline of this picture.
   Write clearly in each of the boxes numbered 1, 2, 3, 4, 5, 6 the type of town represented by the buildings you can see in the picture.

7. Copy the map of Britain. Name all the towns marked with dots and initial letters. Write down one fact about each of these towns.

8. Make a list of the main types of town and write against each type of town the name of an example from the towns of Britain.